CW00421097

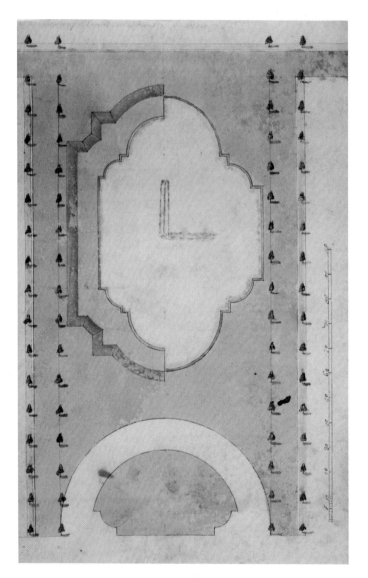

'The Sweeps Canal, in ye Front of the Moor' (S.R.R.C. 2705/105).
Moor Park lies just outside Ludlow. This plan, showing alternative proposals for
a 200 foot (61 metre) long parterre with fountain, is unsigned, but is in the style
of George London (active 1681-1714). London, also a celebrated nurseryman,
was one of the last great designers of formal gardens in the French taste.

Historic Parks

Gardens of Shropshire

by Paul Stamper

**Shropshire
Books**

Front cover: Garden in Dogpole, Shrewsbury, about 1700 (Shrewsbury Civic Society)
Back cover: 19th-century view of Otaheite, Hawkstone (S.R.R.C. 3600/1/40)
© Paul Stamper 1996

Archaeology Service

Information & Community Services

ISBN: 0-903802-70-8

Cover and book design: Paul Brasenell

Managing Editor: Helen Sample

Published by Shropshire Books,

the publishing division of Shropshire County Council's

Information & Community Services Department.

Printed in Great Britain by Livesey Ltd.

Contents

About The Author

Paul Stamper works for Shropshire County Council's Archaeology and Museums Services. Previously, for more than a decade, he was an assistant editor of the *Victoria History of Shropshire*, researching and writing sections of the volumes on Telford, Corvedale and the county's agricultural history. He has also published *The Farmer Feeds Us All* (1989) and (with Robin Hill) *The Working Countryside 1862-1945* (1993), and is a contributor to the *New Dictionary of National Biography*. He is a visiting lecturer in the Department of Archaeology, University of Bristol, and a tutor for the Department of Continuing Education, University of Birmingham.

Originally a digging archaeologist, his many other publications include a report on a major ten-season campaign of excavations at Wharram Percy, North Yorkshire. He is a Fellow of the Society of Antiquaries and secretary of the Society for Medieval Archaeology.

Preface

This study owes much of its detail to work undertaken by the Archaeology Service of Shropshire County Council between 1993 and 1996 on the county's historic parks and gardens for two agencies: Shropshire County Council (Environment Department) and English Heritage. That work produced two archive reports, available in the principal libraries and record repositories in Shropshire and in the National Monuments Record, Swindon. The first report, *A Survey of Historic Parks and Gardens in Shropshire* (S.C.C. Archaeology Unit Report 41, 1993), was a desktop study which identified and briefly described some 280 individual sites, while the second, *Historic Parks and Gardens in Shropshire: A Compendium of Site Reports Compiled 1994-6* (S.C.C. Archaeology Service Report 55, 1996), comprised more detailed studies of fifty or so of the more interesting of those sites incorporating the results of investigations into estate papers and observations made during site visits.

Initiation of, and support for that work owes much to Harley Thomas (Shropshire County Council) and Dr. Harriet Jordan (English Heritage). Ruth Bagley and the staff of the Shropshire Records and Research Centre afforded every assistance and put up with the rather promiscuous rifling of sources that study of the landscape requires. Many other friends have contributed, in some cases very considerably, both to the above-mentioned studies and to this book, with ideas, information, and by reading sections of text. They include Kate Andrew, Andrew Arrol, George Baugh, Tony Carr, Bill Champion, Belinda Cousens, Bob Cromarty, Julian Gibbs, Keith Goodway, James Lawson, Christine Sheard, Alan Snell, Barrie Trinder, and Mike Watson. David Jones kindly helped with the index. I would also like to acknowledge those individuals and institutions who allowed pictorial matter in their ownership to be reproduced here. Individual credits are given in the lists of plates and figures. If, inadvertently and I suspect inevitably, I am guilty of error or omission, I apologize.

My final thanks must be to those owners of Shropshire's historic parks and gardens, and their agents and representatives, who proved so very generous in allowing me access to their properties and in discussing them with me. It must be stressed that mention of a site in this book implies no right of public access, although quite a number are open at least once or twice a year.

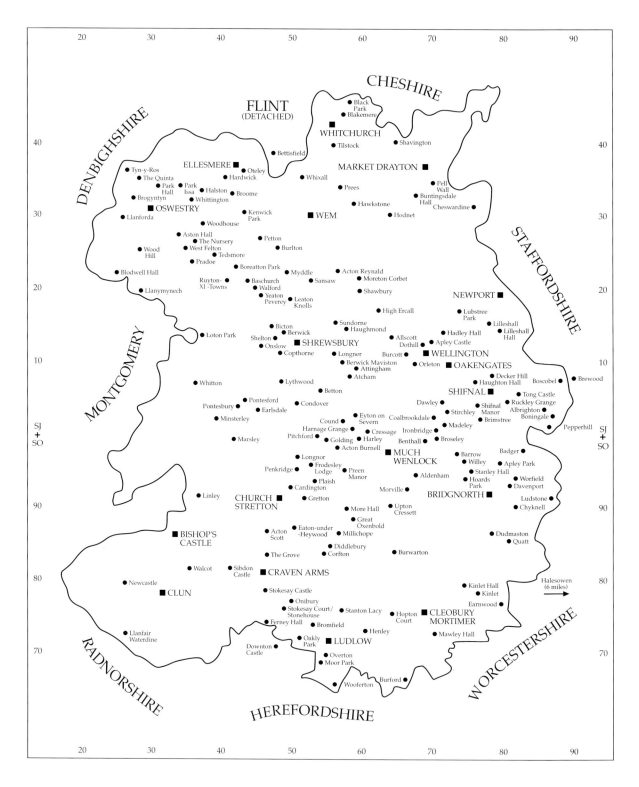

Shropshire, showing parks and gardens mentioned in the text.

Introduction

Despite the long history of garden making and of writing on the philosophy and practicalities of the subject, the formal study of garden history is a very recent development. Indeed, it is only really since the Second World War that it has become a legitimate and increasingly well-defined and self-contained field of inquiry, with links to many other disciplines, from art and literature, whose fashions may (or may not) have influenced those who created gardens, to the more scientific areas of botany, archaeology, and architecture.

Just how recent a phenomenon garden history is can be seen by an examination of the subject's bibliography. What are now seen as the two foundations of the study of garden history, Frank Clark's *The English Landscape Garden* and Christopher Hussey's *English Gardens and Landscapes 1700-1750* , came out in 1948 and 1967. That period also saw the first scholarly biographies of garden designers, Dorothy Stroud's studies of Humphry Repton (1962) and Capability Brown (1975), and the formation (in 1965) of the Garden History Society. Over the next generation the subject moved on apace, abroad as well as in the British Isles, to such an extent that in 1986 Oxford University Press was able to publish an authoritative *Oxford Companion to Gardens* bringing together much of the work in summary form. More modest, but indispensable, was Michael Symes's *Glossary of Garden History* (1993), which did much to establish semantic guidelines in a field strewn with

Fig. 1:
Oakly Park, Bromfield.
A garden and park with
a long and rich history.
The house probably began
as a royal hunting lodge for
which building accounts
of 1552-53 survive
in London's Public
Record Office.

difficulties even for the experienced garden historian; here probably is as near as we will get to differentiating between a belvedere, a gazebo, a pavilion, and a summerhouse! Mention must also be made of the foundation in 1978 of the National Council for the Conservation of Plants and Gardens (N.C.C.P.G.) as a charitable trust devoted to the conservation of ornamental plant cultivars. Shropshire has a county branch, and holds several of the national collections of species, hybrids, and cultivars.

Of necessity much of that early work on garden history was selective, concentrating on what was already known or hinted at, readily available materials, and the few well known names. That base now being established it has been possible to move forward, to be both more comprehensive in what is studied, and through this to be more critical in the conclusions arrived at. That movement, which might be thought of as the second phase of garden history's development, has been made possible mainly by the greatly expanded range of estate papers now available for study in public record offices. The plans and accounts contained therein have laid bare the history of probably several thousand parks and gardens, and thereby brought back once more to public attention designers, contractors and gardeners, in their day figures of not inconsiderable repute but since forgotten. Here one thinks of people such as William Emes (1730-1803), mentioned, if at all, as 'a follower of Capability Brown' but now recognized as probably the leading later 18th-century landscape architect, at least in terms of the number of commissions, in the marches and west midlands.

As the range of source materials has expanded, so too has the chronological range of the subject, and medieval, Renaissance, and 20th-century gardens are now just as much studied as the Arcadian 'natural style' landscapes which Brown and Repton contrived in the later 18th and early 19th centuries. One other major development of the last twenty years has been methodological, as archaeologists began to take an interest in gardens, part and parcel of the growth of 'landscape history' in the wake of W.G. Hoskins's seminal work on *The Making of the English Landscape* (1957).

Fig. 2:
Netley Hall,
the gothick lodge
of 1826.

That interest has been important for two reasons. Firstly archaeologists were used to looking at, and 'reading' the landscape, and especially often minor earthworks, and combining those observations with the results of more conventional research in muniment rooms and record offices. More recently excavation has begun to be routinely used to investigate individual gardens, whether - as in the walled kitchen garden at Acton Scott - at a very simplistic level by using trenches to locate and assess the condition of paths or flower beds, or in a few instances in large excavations, as heroic as any in the rural landscape, where enlightenment is sought about much broader aspects of what is perhaps a very large garden with a complex history. Kirby Hall, in Northamptonshire, saw one of the first exercises of that kind, followed in the early 1990s by the laying bare of the17th-century king's 'privy', or private garden at Hampton Court Palace.

Historic parks and gardens had not gone unremarked by Shropshire historians. Several dozen have received at least passing mention in parish histories written for the *Victoria County History*, while others have been noticed in family or house histories. Individual commissions have also been cited in biographical studies, such as those by Dorothy Stroud, of the works of individual designers, or in period overviews such as Brent Elliott's of the Victorian garden[1] or David Jacques's of the Georgian.[2] Probably the nearest there has been until now in the way of a county summary were sections of Trevor Rowley's 1972 volume on Shropshire in the *Making of the English Landscape* series which also included several maps of parks redrawn from originals in the county record office.

Systematic work on Shropshire's historic parks and gardens began only in the 1990s when the County Council, assisted by the Countryside Commission, commissioned a desk-based survey and gazetteer which identified some 280 landscapes which appeared to have qualities which marked them out as notable.[3] Subsequently almost fifty of those were studied in greater detail, with site visits and work on estate papers in the record office.[4] Copies of both those reports are lodged with the Shropshire Records and Research Centre in Shrewsbury. To no small extent they form the basis of this book which, it must be stressed, makes no claims to be the last word on the subject.

Fig.3:
Cabbages, a staple vegetable in the Middle Ages and later.
This 1629 engraving shows 1. Close Cabbage 2. Open Cabbage
3. Curled Savoy Colewort 4. Cole Flower 5. Curled Colewort
6. Changeable Curled Colewort 7. Cole Rape
8. Unnamed, perhaps Kohl Rabi.

Medieval and Renaissance

'... with the kingdom made safe on all sides ... the most kindly Edward passed his life in security and peace, and spent much of his time in the glades and woods in the pleasures of hunting. After divine service, which he gladly and devoutly attended every day, he took much pleasure in hawks and birds of that kind which were brought before him, and was really delighted by the baying and scrambling of the hounds. In these and such like activities he sometimes spent the day, and it was in these alone that he seemed naturally inclined to snatch some worldly pleasure.'[1]

Thus, writing within a year of his death in 1066 and with memory still fresh, the latter years of Edward the Confessor were recalled by his monk biographer. Although later revered chiefly for his piety Edward was in fact a robust and forceful king, a half-Viking who came to the throne in 1042 when nearly forty years old after a life spent largely in exile in Normandy. His love of hunting, which was shared by many later rulers of England, was not just of a thrilling sport. The chase offered valuable practice in the arts of war: of handling a horse at speed across rough terrain, all day long and in every kind of weather, while at the same time devising tactics and giving orders designed to bring a quarry to bay. It demanded, moreover, a proficiency with weapons, again while horsed, and considerable courage. These were the things that made it the sport of kings.

While Domesday Book records a royal hunting park at Marsley, north of the Stiperstones,[2] most hunting was probably across open countryside. The same source states that whenever Edward the Confessor came to Shrewsbury it was the custom for the 'better' townsmen who had horses to guard him as he hunted and for the sheriff to supply 36 men on foot to 'stall' game, acting as drivers and beaters. Although the most dangerous, and thus highly regarded, beast of the chase was the boar, deer provided the usual quarry, and to guarantee their availability they were apparently kept and bred in enclosures called hays. Domesday Book records 36 of these in Shropshire, most of them in the south-west quarter of the county; that at Corfton was described specifically to be for the catching of roe deer.[3]

Under the Norman kings the right to hunt deer was almost exclusively reserved by the Crown; huge areas were deemed to be 'forest', that is subject to the special regulations of Forest Law with its nominally draconian penalties for those who harmed the king's deer. For at least a century after the Conquest only begrudgingly did the Crown grant the right to hold private hunting grounds - parks and chases - to others.

Shropshire's first parks are poorly documented and were probably anyway few in number.[4]
In 1195 John le Strange (II) enlarged his park at Ruyton, while on the county boundary the Bishop
of Coventry was permitted in 1206 to make a leap to allow deer to enter his park at Brewood.
In the later 13th century the number of parks began to increase rapidly as the Crown became more
willing to grant licences for their construction, not least because such grants had to be bought and
represented a valuable source of income for the king. Fines when the system was deemed to have
been bypassed could be even more lucrative, as in 1251 when the Prior of Wenlock had to pay the
huge sum of £200 to retain his unlicensed park at Oxenbold, in Corvedale. In Shropshire at least
25 parks were created between 1270 and 1310, most of them of 50-100 acres although some were
larger. At Acton Burnell 70 acres of Cumbes wood were imparked in 1270 by Robert Burnell,
Bishop of Bath and Wells and Chancellor of England, to which 60 acres were added in 1280.
By 1290 three deer leaps, which allowed deer to enter the park but not to leave it, had been
constructed, and by 1292 the park also contained fish ponds. Within a century the park pale had
been replaced by a wall, at least on its south side. The expenditure on a park, therefore, both in
setting up and running it, was likely to be considerable. As well as a licence to establish the park
the Crown might also demand, as at Shawbury in 1253,[5] payment if a deer leap was constructed.
In addition compensation might have to be provided, either in cash or by the provision of rights
in lieu, where common rights were extinguished. At Hodnet, for instance, in 1275, an inquest
determined that Sir Odo of Hodnet could inclose two footpaths which ran through the centre
of his park provided he established new routes around the park in their place.[6]

As the example of Acton Burnell shows, it was not only the laity who enjoyed the hunt,
although clergymen and monks usually excused themselves by saying that they needed hunting
parks in order to entertain important guests. In 1338 the Bishop of Coventry and Lichfield
reprimanded the Prioress of White Ladies Priory, near Brewood, for hunting and keeping hounds,

Fig. 4:
White Ladies Priory,
as painted in 1791 by Revd. Williams.
In 1338 its prioress was reprimanded
for hunting.

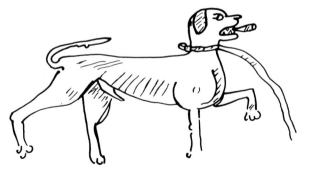

Fig. 5:
A talbot, or hunting dog, drawn on a deed
of 1480 belonging to Lilleshall Abbey.
Usually white or light coloured these
heavy-jawed animals were used both to track
and hunt, and had great powers of scent.

while at Haughmond Abbey in 1355 the main fault was said to be the canons' love of hunting, for which they kept special horses.[7] These were expensive indulgences, and not only because of the costs of maintaining a park and buying and stabling horses. Dogs, and special servants too were needed. At Cleobury Mortimer in 1328 a pack of 86 dogs seems to have been maintained by the Earl of March, 26 of them harriers and the rest hounds. These dogs, sufficiently important to be guarded by pages, were fed twice a day, first with coarse bread and in the evening with bran made into a mash or porridge.[8]

Those examples notwithstanding, parks which actually saw organized hunting may have been in the minority, and many apparently operated purely as deer reserves, from which animals could be taken by the lord's representative as required. The gift of deer, whether as haunches of venison or live, as in the 1290s when the Prior of Wenlock's park at Madeley was restocked with royal deer,[9] was a well understood act of patronage. Red and roe deer are both native to the British Isles, whereas fallow deer, well suited as parkland animals because they will graze alongside cattle and because they may fatten better on poor land than red deer, were a Norman introduction. At Blakemere in 1540 the park contained both red and fallow deer,[10] but in general indications of the type of deer present are rare; Oliver Rackham believes the vast majority of park deer would have been fallow.[11] More frequent are indications of how difficult it was to manage a park successfully, and at Wem in 1281 the uninclosed park contained no beasts of the chase and the inclosed park just eleven.[12]

On the whole, until at least the later 16th century, parks rarely adjoined the houses of their owners. Rather they were usually sited towards the edges of estates, on wooded or perhaps poor quality land. Nevertheless, if well managed, they could produce a useful income whether in cash or kind, from a range of diversified, yet specialist, farming activities. Many parks were home to studs, and in the early 14th century there were horses at all three of the Earl of Arundel's parks at Oswestry and Bromhurst,[13] while in 1328 that at Clun held over 160 horses.[14] Oxen, too, might be raised in the lord's park, and in the 1350s some belonging to the Stranges were rustled from Black park near Whitchurch and taken into Cheshire,[15] while in 1315 deer, 24 mares, 16 colts and 80 oxen were stolen from Myddle park.[16] Such numbers seem plausible, whereas the claims of Fulk Fitzwarren in 1331 that malefactors had broken into Whittington park and driven off 5 horses, 100 mares, 100 colts, 48 oxen, 40 bullocks, 40 heifers, 500 sheep and 100 swine, and also fished his stews, hunted his deer and chopped down timber,[17] would seem to demand further investigation. In 1298 wild swine were reported to have been stolen from Cound park; these too may have been kept as much as beasts of the chase as for their meat, for the challenge and danger a boar presented to the hunter made the animal much respected.[18] Parks were also a suitably secure environment within which to establish a warren where, as at Woofferton in 1337,[19] rabbits, hares, partridges, pheasants and the like could be reared, and in 1374 the parker at Earnwood, near Kinlet, had to paint the park trees with tar to prevent them being barked by the rabbits.[20] As time went on this diversification within parks became more noticeable, and more and more people were like Sir Charles Foxe who in 1617 had 'more sheep and cattle than deer' in his park at Oakly, near Bromfield.[21]

Most parks were a mixture of open grass 'lawns' and woodland. Some of the woodland might be managed as coppice, and kept well fenced to protect it from animals, although the classic parkland form of wood management was pollarding. Here crops of wood were taken every ten years or so from trees which had been cut off 2-3 metres above the ground, the young wood growing out of the reach of browsing animals. It may be pollarding, for instance, which is indicated by mid 16th-century leases of Minsterley park which included the right to lop trees for cattle food.[22]

Although historical sources often refer to gardens and orchards more detailed records, at least in Shropshire, are unusual. A tantalizing glimpse of what has been lost is provided by a chance reference to the acquisition of spades from Sheffield for the gardener at the Talbot's important moated house at Blakemere, near Whitchurch.[23] That adjoined Blakemere Pool,[24] just as at Oxenbold (Plate 2) the Prior of Wenlock's country manor house of the 1240s[25] was situated next to and overlooking a great fishpool. In both instances the positioning was probably deliberate, with the water intended to provide an aesthetically pleasing setting for the house. If so these sites bear comparison with Clun Castle, where a great water garden or *pleasance* was constructed in the later Middle Ages (Plate 4). Until the 1540s Clun was the main seat in the Marches of the FitzAlans, earls of Arundel, who in the later 13th and 14th centuries apparently remodelled the castle to make it less a military stronghold and more a place of recreation. New accommodation was provided by a huge four-storey lodgings block - visitors included Edward I in 1295 and Edward III who came to hunt in 1362 - and a new setting for the castle by the *pleasance*. Air photography suggests that its main elements were an artificial lake and a large rectangular island with an internal pond. On the island there were probably lawns, sweet smelling flowers and one or more bowers, the whole providing a picturesque and romantic retreat for the Arundels and their guests from the communal life of the castle, a place to enjoy a more private existence, and perhaps to boat and fish. Such water gardens have now been recognized at a number of major castles and manor houses including Leeds Castle (Kent), where a 'gloriet' or island palace was built for Eleanor of Castile in 1278-90, and Kenilworth Castle (Warws.), where a *pleasance* was built for Henry V in 1414-17.[26]

It was not only the mighty who found water an attractive adjunct to their houses. From the 13th century ordinary lords of manors increasingly chose to enclose their manor houses, and sometimes their farm buildings, gardens and orchards too, with moats; well over 150 Shropshire examples are now known. The reason, at least in part, was probably for security, for when combined with a good thorn hedge a moat provided some security against thieves and cattle rustlers. Moats also had other functions, for instance serving as fishponds, and in 1735 it was (improbably) claimed that the moat at Ludstone Hall contained 1,000 carp, 1,000 tench and 1,000 perch.[27] Nevertheless, that a moat provided an attractive setting for a house, one moreover that echoed the moated castles of the great and the good, still probably played its part. Such sentiments, for instance, perhaps lay behind the creation of the extraordinary, and complex, group of earthworks which adjoins the Court House, at Gretton, near Cardington. The site appears to lack an identity - unusually it cannot be associated with a particular house or estate - but it has been suggested that it represents the remains of a late medieval or early post-medieval house surrounded by a narrow moat or ditch and set about with shallow lakes, fishponds, and channels in what was principally an ornamental landscape.[28]

Unfortunately very little is known for sure of the gardens which would have existed at the various monasteries in the county where herbs and medicinal plants would have been grown among more functional fruits and vegetables. Excavations at Haughmond Abbey did find traces of a garden in the

Fig. 6:
An early 19th-century drawing of Ludstone Hall.
The parapet of the bridge across the moat can be seen
between the gate piers and the house.

cloister, with triangular coping stones from a wall re-used to mark out a bed around the edge of what may have been a lawn, but this has been dated to about 1600, by when the monastery had been converted by the Barker family into a country house.[29]

Although in the late 17th century John Aubrey was to claim that it was 'in the time of King Charles the Second [that] gardening was much improved and became common', the same sentiment had been expressed a century earlier by William Harrison. 'Within these forty years', he wrote in the 1570s, 'if you look into our gardens annexed to our houses, how wonderfully is their beauty increased, not only with flowers ... and variety of curious and costly workmanship, but also with rare and medicinable herbs ... so that in comparison of this present, the ancient gardens were but dung-hills'.[30]

The first great garden of which a pictorial representation survives is also one of the finest: Shifnal Manor.[31] Here, in the 1590s, the Earl of Shrewsbury began a programme of repairs and improvements. In the dining room, for instance, he raised the ceiling to 21 feet and installed a great gable-end window, considered by his steward to be 'the stateliest window of timber I ever did see'. By 1635 (Plates 5-6) equally grand gardens had been created on the ground which falls away from the spur-top house: a series of walled and terraced gardens and parterres with low clipped box hedges and bushes and, beyond, a formal canal and a wilderness. The elaborate patterns of the garden were best appreciated from above, either from the upper floors of the house or from the gazebo or banqueting house at the end of the main walled compartment. At their very centre was a heart-shaped pond, an emblem of Catholic sympathies. Unfortunately this provides little indication of for whom the gardens were created. Both the Earl of Shrewsbury, who in the early 1590s was said to be surrounded by 'notorious papists and dangerous recusants', and Anne Dacre, Dowager Countess of Arundel (d. 1630), his son-in-law's mother who moved to Shifnal at some stage after 1616, were supporters of the Old Faith. Whichever the creator, such a garden was in the very van of fashion.

Not dissimilar to those at Shifnal may have been the gardens at Eyton on Severn, where about 1607 Sir Francis Newport built a great new house overlooking the floodplain of the River Severn. All trace of that building, which reputedly resembled Condover Hall and which was burnt down in the mid 18th century, has now gone, but what do survive are its two banqueting houses, probably also of about 1607. These lay at the corners of the main walled garden, each comprising an octagonal sandstone and brick building of two storeys, the lower floor left open, loggia-style.

Fig. 7:
One of the banqueting houses at Eyton on Severn, as drawn by David Parkes in 1814. The roof of the stair turret of the second can be seen beyond.

Access to the upper room, which had a fireplace and three large windows, and to the balustraded flat roof was via a three-storey stair turret, also octagonal, roofed with a lead cupola. Here, as at Shifnal, the family and their guests could retire after banquets to enjoy desserts, confectionery, and entertainment as they looked out over the formal gardens to the world beyond. One of the banqueting houses is now incorporated in Eyton on Severn Farmhouse but the other, restored in the 1980s by the Vivat Trust, survives in excellent condition and gives some idea of the size and quality of Sir Francis Newport's great mansion complex.[32]

A contemporary garden of at least equal scale and importance lay to the south of the Corbets' splendid new Renaissance house at Moreton Corbet. That garden, traces of which can be seen as earthworks, was perhaps constructed as part of improvements at Moreton Corbet of the late 1570s and was overlooked from a first-floor gallery and probably a walk on the leads. When surveyed in 1588 the garden covered about two acres, 'in the middle of which ... are divers solars (the latin word used by the scribe is *solaria*) cut into one rock, and on the south side of the garden is a small house called a keep for the use of the gardener, and a well for watering the garden, and there are divers covered walks and arbours.' Another grand house of the late 16th century was Condover Hall, built in the 1580s and 1590s for the lawyer Thomas Owen.[33] His wide culture and erudition were reflected in his new house, which while of traditional Tudor H-plan incorporated a number of more advanced Renaissance features including a loggia - an open cloister or arcade - on the south-west, garden, front. Above the loggia, as at Moreton, was a long gallery overlooking the main garden, where in 1598, as work on the new house was nearing completion, the great walk was turfed and a bowling alley laid out.[34]

Sadly no survey such as that for Moreton survives from Condover to give more detail about what must have been very sumptuous gardens, nor from Apley Park where in 1647 the gardens included a banqueting house with a carpet, table board, and six stools.[35] Similarly undocumented is the landscape around Madeley Court where there are hints that the gardens, enclosed with brick walls in the 17th century, matched the quality of the turreted gatehouse. Virtually all that survives at Madeley, in the centre of the garden, is an elaborate stone sundial and astronomical toy. There was a great interest in such contrivances in the early 17th century, both as technical devices and as symbolic reminders, set in gardens designed for relaxation and contemplation, of the passage of time. A particularly early and fine example stood on the terrace at Park Hall, near Oswestry, dated 1578 and carrying not only seven dials but also verse in latin.[36] Another intricate example is shown on a painting of about 1700 of a garden in Dogpole, Shrewsbury,[37] a more conventional

Fig. 8:
The 'arber' at Dothill,
as depicted in 1626.
Sturdy posts and a staircase
help support the tree houses.

Plate 1: The deer park at Chetwynd. Although a post-medieval creation it closely resembles earlier parks, a mixture of open grassland with individual mature trees and denser areas of woodland.

Plate 2 (above): Great Oxenbold.
A country manor house of the priors of Wenlock,
built in the 1240s. It overlooked a great fishpond.

Plate 3 (left): A Flemish nobleman's garden of the late 15th century. Here are many elements of later medieval gardens, such as compartments defined by walls and trellises, raised beds, turf benches, and shady fruit trees. At the heart of the garden are an ornamental fountain and rill.

Plate 4: The pleasance at Clun Castle. Right of the winding, tree-lined river is the site of the FitzAlans' water garden. Infilled ditches and ponds remain lush and dark green while the rest of the crop ripens.

Plate 5 (above): The gazebo at Shifnal Manor. Clearly shown on the 1635 map at the end of the main garden compartment, this was a very fashionable building, built partly of brick. From the main, upper room, both the gardens and the landscape beyond could be admired.

Plate 6 (right): The Manor, Shifnal, in 1635. Typically for this date the cartographer has used a bird's eye view. Surviving details suggest this is a very accurate representation of the complex.

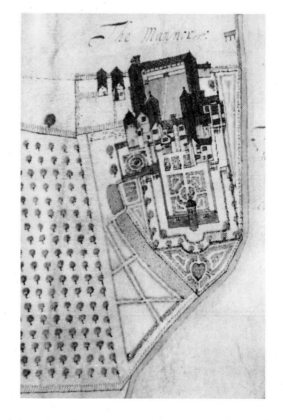

one on a drawing of Dothill in 1626,[38] and at Lilleshall Old Hall there was one dated 1630.[39] Others are still to be found in gardens and churchyards throughout the county, often datable by an inscription on the dial.

Symbolism of a different sort may also have lain behind the construction of tree houses at Pitchford and Dothill, which probably reflects the cult of melancholy which became fashionable in court and intellectual circles in late Elizabethan England. Melancholy, one of the four humours, came to be seen as a mark of genius, capable of making men witty and, Robert Burton claimed, 'excellent Philosophers, Poets, Prophets, etc.'[40] As Sir Roy Strong has pointed out, such men sought out as places for solitary meditation not the walks of a formal garden but the shade of the greenwood tree and the solace of a babbling brook, and as the fashion spread, bowers, arbours and even artificial wildernesses began to be built outside formal gardens. Dothill, near Wellington, where by 1626 an 'arber' had been constructed about 250 metres east of the house, would seem to be an early example of the cult. That arbour actually comprised a pair of rustic bowers, lodged in a single tree and set about by timber staging and stairs.[41] The date of the Pitchford example, present by 1714,[42] is unknown, but it too lies at some remove from the main house, in the branches of a massive lime tree. Unfortunately its original form is unknown. Its present appearance and gothick plastered interior, which in 1783 was embellished with 'landscape painting of the adjoining country' around the tops of the walls,[43] are largely the result of modernization in the later 18th century.

One amusement which the greater 16th- and 17th-century Shropshire gardens may have contained was a maze. In England they first appear in the Tudor period, laid out in turf or in low growing shrubs and herbs, with hedge mazes being a later 17th-century development. No specific examples are documented from Shropshire houses, although it is known that by the 1570s the Shoemakers, one of Shrewsbury's trade guilds, had a turf maze next to their bower - what we would today call a clubhouse - on Kingsland, just outside the town.[44] In the late 18th century and before its destruction in the early 19th when a windmill was built on the site, shoemakers would race through it, the winner jumping to place his heels in the eyes of an exaggerated human head cut in the centre.[45]

Perhaps the most innovative garden in the county in the 17th century was at Llanforda, west of Oswestry, where botanical experiments were carried out alongside fish farming.[46] The medium-sized Llanforda estate was inherited in 1634 by Edward Lloyd, then aged about 25, who apparently set about developing the gardens, which by the 1640s may have rivalled the celebrated ones at the nearby Hanmer. Riotous in his habits, sequestration after the Civil War further reduced his fortunes. On returning home in 1645 he wrote to his mother, apparently chastened, that Llanforda had changed. No longer could he be patron to poets and harpists; now his only ambition was to rebuild his estate and to worship God in his garden. 'I have been charged', he noted ruefully, 'with folly for my gardens and walks, for my wilderness and fountain and you dear mother have been distant with me for them as to the charges, and the charges charges them with vanity: 'tis true ... there is not such a noble and gentleman like vanity ... as gardens and walks.'

Although the estate inherited by Lloyd's son in 1653, also Edward, was heavily indebted, the gardens were kept up. Seeds, including cucumber, melon, asparagus, cauliflower and artichoke were regularly purchased from London suppliers including Edward Fuller, the capital's leading seedsman, although Lloyd claimed his own stock was superior. Indeed, there is some evidence that Llanforda's kitchen and fruit gardens were operating as a market garden at this time. In the later 1670s the pleasure grounds and the physic garden were under improvement, and letters of 1677-8 speak of work in the wilderness and especially of the pleasure Lloyd got from the snowdrops which grew there. His eye for detail was considerable: a plant pot, for instance, was adorned with his motto, painted in gold. Much of the work at this time was presumably undertaken by Samson, the newly arrived negro gardener.

A new and more scientific era of gardening began at Llanforda in 1679-80 with the employment of the highly respected botanist and gardener Edward Morgan, whose earlier responsibilities had included the Westminster Medical Garden. With him came two or more students of botany, whose experiments included comparing the growth rates of plants in London and Shropshire. Seeds were obtained from Oxford as well as London, and plant collecting forays were made into Montgomeryshire and north Wales. Given this level of gardening activity it is perhaps not surprising that Lloyd's financial troubles continued, and in the 1680s he offered an interest in the estate to Lady Herbert of Powys Castle. She would have 'the absolute command of my house during my life, the tulip garden, pigeonhouse garden, parlour garden, wilderness, lower garden and well, the command of my fishponds and a key for herself to the physick garden and the fruit garden beyond the nursery.'

Only the kitchen garden walls, now partly collapsed, survived Llanforda's demolition in the years after 1940. But in the surrounding fields is other evidence of the Lloyds' remarkable 17th-century enterprise. In the1660s the younger Edward began to invest in the expanding north Welsh fishing industry, renting a fishery on the River Dovey. The sources also suggest that he was breeding freshwater fish, and that is presumably the explanation for the twenty or so fishponds, mostly now dry, in the vicinity of the former house. In its heyday, Llanforda must have been one of the most remarkable places in the county.

Nevertheless, it was far from the only garden of renown. One of the Lloyds' acquaintances would almost certainly have been John Rea of Kinlet, author, nurseryman, and grower of flowers.[47] Born about 1600 he took up gardening in his twenties, and by the 1650s had an established reputation as a grower of 'exquisite' flowers, notably tulips, of which he offered 200 varieties, and carnations. Other stock included 31 varieties of roses and 44 of plums. Although he was careful to define himself as a grower of flowers and not a maker of gardens, he did even so design at least one garden, for Charles Gerard, fourth Baron Gerard, for his house at Gerard's Bromley (Staffs.), and discussed garden design in his *Complete Floriledge*, published in 1665. That describes at some length shrubs, climbers, bulbs and other plants for flower and fruit 'gardens of delight', with the rarer and choicer examples being reserved for the former. Rea also specified what he considered to be the ideal garden plan for a gentleman, with flower and fruit gardens close to the house and the kitchen gardens at some remove. The flower garden was recommended to be 20 yards square, and to comprise an outer alley or walk divided by wooden rails and low, evergreen hedges from a central 'fret', an elaborately patterned complex of flower beds bordered with beaten sand alleys. On one side of the garden was to be an octagonal summerhouse 'finely painted with landscapes and other conceits' containing a table and seats; this would serve not only as a place of 'delight and entertainment' but also, more mundanely, as somewhere to sit and label such things as tulip bulbs.

On Rea's death in 1681 his plant collection passed to his son-in-law Samuel Gilbert, rector of Quatt and chaplain to Jane, Baroness Gerard, whose garden Rea had replanned over fifteen years before.[48] Unfortunately Gilbert was abroad at the time, and before his return some of the tulip collection, said to be the largest of any man in England, was lost. Even so, over a hundred types survived. Gilbert was evidently no mean florist in his own right, and in 1682 published *The florists vade-mecum*. Reading this it is apparent that his own favourite flower was the auricula, and Gilbert claimed to have the finest collection of them in the county.

Fig. 9:
The title page of John Rea's Flora of 1665.
Flora, flanked by vases of cut flowers,
is seated on the pediment with Ceres (left)
and Pomona below. The cost of printing
caused Rea to exclude all illustrations
of flowers in the text itself.

Fig. 10:
A head-piece
(engraved by Frederik Hendrik van Hove)
from page 1 of Rea's Flora.
Dutch flower paintings
were highly popular
in 17th-century England.

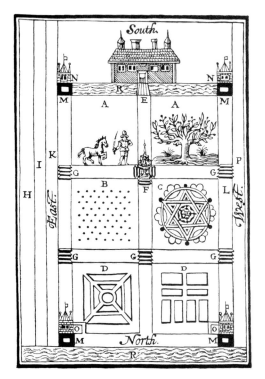

Fig. 11 (left):
A compartmentalized garden design from
William Lawson's 'A New Orchard and Garden' (1618).
The man and horse stand in a forecourt, with beyond
an orchard, fruit garden, and compartments with
vegetable beds. The garden has a fountain, stairs,
and four summerhouses.

Fig. 12 (below):
Boscobel and its surrounding landscape,
redrawn about 1800 from Hollar's
original drawing of about 1660.

Compartmentalized gardens such as Rea advocated, containing formal and symmetrical beds, can be glimpsed on many of the surviving 17th-century maps and plans of Shropshire houses, such as that of Aldenham in 1625.[49] At Condover in the 1650s Sir Roger Owen seems to have concentrated most of his soft fruits including vines in the south walk, noting in 1657 that on 18 May he gathered a pint-and-a-half of strawberries and that his apricots were ripe by the beginning of July.[50] There are more modest compartments at one of the county's best known historic gardens, Boscobel, where Charles II hid in 1651 as he fled after the battle of Worcester. About 1660 Boscobel was drawn by Wenceslas Hollar, his view showing the gardens to be very much as they are today, with a mount and arbour (like the tree houses at Dothill and Pitchford a place for contemplation) providing a view over the several small formal beds and out to the landscape beyond. Early in the 17th century the house had been remodelled as a hunting lodge, and it was presumably to keep deer out of the garden that the tall palisade had been built around it. Hollar's drawing, however, shows that beyond the garden was an octagonal table, where the company could dine in a pleasing and scenic woodland setting on the edge of Boscobel wood.[51]

How exceptional such an aesthetic appreciation of landscape beyond the pleasure ground would have been at this time is difficult to say, but that it did exist has already been suggested in the discussion of the gazebo at Shifnal, the banqueting house at Eyton, and the tree houses. It is further demonstrated by evidence given during a court case in 1615 concerning depredations on the manor of Pepperhill by its tenants. They, it was said, had 'topped, cropped, and lopped' about 100 great oaks in the park, which 'were never topped, cropped or lopped before, but continually kept and preserved both for the beauty of the park and [to] safeguard the ... house from the extremity of the weather ...'.[52] It was presumably also at least in part the beauty of parks which led in the 17th century to the construction of raised viewpoints on lodges, whether, as at Lilleshall, a balcony[53] or,

Fig. 13:
Harnage Grange, Cound, the gazebo.
Probably built by the Fowlers
who were adding to the property after
1569, this is a fine example of this type
of garden building. Gazebo, popularly
derived from the latin 'I shall gaze',
reflects the importance of the upper room
in such buildings, from which a view
of the gardens could be enjoyed.

as at Frodesley, a roof-top platform.[54] Prospect mounds, too, were probably far more common than the number surviving today would suggest. As well as that at Boscobel examples are evidenced at More Hall, in Shipton, in 1664,[55] and at Blodwell Hall.[56] Another example of landscape appreciation relates to the visit of Charles I to Bridgnorth in 1642, when he reputedly walked in the vicinity of the castle specifically to admire the view which he observed was 'as pleasant a walk as any in his kingdom.'[57]

By the later 16th century the concept of the park was changing. Increasingly, as at the fashionable brick houses of Upton Cressett (Plate 8) and Plaish, and at Condover, Harnage Grange and Frodesley, deer parks were considered an appropriate setting for a new house. Faced with the reality of their cost, however, an owner's enthusiasm could soon wane. At Shifnal in 1597 the Earl of Shrewsbury's steward reported that 'the deer die in this park at this present and so soon as they be dead the poor folks [of Shifnal] carry them to the town and eat them.' Seven years later parts of the park were being farmed and, with little hay available, over fifty of the 250-strong herd died from lack of feed. The pale was rotting and poachers, including officials from the earl's own household, were a problem. Little wonder that the steward complained of how difficult it was to manage the park honestly.[58] At Kenwick, three miles south of Ellesmere, the struggle to keep the park going seems to have been given up in 1602, by when the park pale was rotting and had sections missing.[59] In that year it was leased to James Croft, who subsequently sublet a third of it in parcels to 23 under tenants attracted by the possibility of making a profit by selling the old park timber as fuel to glassworks.[60] A similar fate met another north Shropshire park, Tilstock, south of Whitchurch. A map of about 1600 shows farmers Gregorie and Chawner among newly felled trees with axes over their shoulders.[61]

Hunting and venison, however, remained potent symbols of lordship and instruments of patronage. Even if against the general trend, parks of the traditional type were still being formed in the 16th and 17th centuries, often by families newly established in county society. At Stokesay, for instance, it was apparently the Vernons who created a 275-acre park just west of the castle in the 16th century,[62] while in 1638 Lord Newport gave deer from High Ercall park to stock Francis Ottley's new park at Pitchford.[63] At much the same time Newport himself was making a park at Cressage, taking in poor quality land inclosed a century earlier out of the great common wood shared by Harley and Cressage.[64] At Willey, near Much Wenlock, its enterprising and ambitious new owner John Weld inclosed some 400 acres in a new park about 1625, arousing envy among his neighbours.[65] Over the next ten years it was surrounded with a pale, stocked with deer and had fishponds dug. Other schemes under consideration in 1631 included the ploughing and flooding of land to improve the quality of the meadow and coppice grounds. From the start Weld was troubled by petty pilferers. In 1636, for instance, Edward Hayward was accused of stealing not only holly bushes - probably as animal feed - from the park but also one of the pales. Poaching, of both deer and fish, was always a more serious problem, and within almost every park there was a lodge, home of the parker who was responsible, like a modern gamekeeper, for the management of the stock and for its protection. Many lodges were moated or otherwise secured, in tacit recognition of the violence that might be directed against the parker whether by poachers, or by those raiding the park as a dramatic gesture against an unpopular lord or neighbour. The latter motive probably lay behind a midnight raid by fourteen men, armed with bows and arrows, crossbows, billhooks and swords, on Sir John Talbot's park at Pepperhill, close to the boundary with Staffordshire, in the mid 16th century. The park keepers, Leonard and John Arne, were shot at and had to retreat to the lodge, the door and thatched roof of which were soon peppered with arrows. The 'warlike and riotous' gang then hunted and killed 20 deer, although only eight were taken away.[66]

Many of the Lodge Farms which are found in the countryside originated as deer park lodges. Where the original house survives it is often little if at all different from a small farmhouse of the period. Others, however, like the Hayes, in Mount Road, Oswestry, a cruciform stone building of the mid 17th century, exhibit an architectural pretension which heralded their owners' status. Presumably in such lodges a parlour would be pressed into use if the lord wished to take refreshment during the hunt or to entertain guests. Some lodges, however, lacked bedchambers and seem to have been more like sylvan banqueting houses, with a first-floor chamber above a ground-floor service area. The best example is in the deer park at Loton (Plate 9). It is a small sandstone building perhaps most easily described as a two-storey tower with porthole-fashion windows and a low pyramidal roof. Inside there are fireplaces on both floors, which are connected by a dog-leg corner staircase, and remains of a high quality decorative scheme including elaborately carved purlins and a red ochre coloured roof. A date of about 1675 seems likely. Another lodge, the Park House, stands on high ground in the deer park at Henley Hall, on the western slopes of Clee Hill. It is of brick, and its principal first-floor room is well lit and has a corner fireplace. Although Listed as of late 18th-century date the distinguished architectural historian Christopher Hussey thought it basically an early 17th-century building, albeit one with Georgian additions.[67] The plan of Penkridge Hall, near Leebotwood, indicates that it too may have been built as a place to take refreshment during the hunt, in this case in the woods around the Lawley Hill. Built in 1590 by Rowland Whitbrook, a Bridgnorth wool merchant, and named after his wife's Staffordshire birthplace, it is an elaborate timber-framed structure, with one main room on each of its two floors.[68]

A larger structure, but perhaps analogous, is Hoards Park, a substantial hilltop farm a mile north of Bridgnorth. This estate, acquired from the Hordes, was one of the largest bought by the Londoner William Whitmore as he began to build up a country estate in the area in the years around 1620. About thirty years later he, or his son or nephew, seems to have transformed the property, cladding the old timber-framed house in brick and enlarging it, and constructing two great brick walled enclosures, one to either side. The smaller, about 80 metres square (Plate 7), was undoubtedly an orchard, and in its walls (as in others nearer the house) are bee boles, arched recesses intended to give shelter to straw bee skeps. Although the connection between bees and fruit pollination was not determined until the mid 18th century, as early as 1618 Lawson had noted that 'bees thrive in an orchard.' The other enclosure, some 250 metres square, enclosed the upper part of a small valley leading down to the River Severn, and was overlooked by a flat-topped spur of land running out from the house for about 75 metres. All the walls are very tall, some 2.5 metres or so, probably to keep deer in or out. It seems likely that what Hoards Park comprised was a pleasant country retreat

Fig. 14:
Onions and turnips,
from John Gerard's
'Herbal' of 1597.

Fig. 15:
An illustration of planting in beds and
the use of the dibble, from the 1652 edition
of Thomas Hill's 'The Gardener's Labyrinth'.
First published in 1577, this was the first
popular book on gardening in English.

for the Whitmores, part country house and part park lodge, with a formal garden (as at Shifnal Manor) running out, on to and around the spur and overlooking an enclosure. In the 1840s the enclosure was called Buck Orchard, and deer may have been kept here before being released to be coursed in the valley beyond.[69]

Almost all of the evidence presented above inevitably concerns the gardens and parks of the well-to-do, that is the record-keeping class. Glimpses of more homely gardens are few and far between, but they are enough to show that apart from the urban poor most people had a garden of sorts. In 1646, for instance, during the Civil War, Cuthbert Hely fled Ludlow for London. On his return he found his Bull Ring properties much abused: a tenant had been frightened off, privy doors barricaded, and his tulips replaced by onions.[70] Vegetable growing, of course, had always been important to those ordinary people fortunate enough to have a garden. But from the mid 16th century dietary habits changed, and commentators such as William Harrison, writing in the 1580s, began to note how vegetables had become an important part of the diet of every Englishman, no matter how humble. In 1599 a Shrewsbury dyer, Richard Gardiner, published *Profitable instructions for the manuring, sowing and planting of kitchin* (sic) *gardens*, the first book in English devoted entirely to the cultivation of vegetables. Dedicated to his 'loving neighbours and friends within Shrewsbury', a second edition appeared in 1603.[71] The book contains advice, particularly for the benefit of the poor (for whom Gardiner had set up a soup kitchen during the famine of the 1590s)[72] on how to grow produce such as carrots, cabbages, parsnips, lettuce, beans, onions, turnips, cucumbers, melons (or pompons), gourds, and artichokes. Gardiner was especially keen to promote the cultivation of carrots, and rebuked the English for not growing more of them. Potatoes are not mentioned, for although they were not unknown as a garden crop before 1600 they remained rare and costly until the mid 17th century. Although a man of substance Gardiner was clearly a diligent, observant and most of all practical vegetable gardener, whose advice on techniques and varieties was well founded on long-standing personal, and (perhaps as his surname suggests), family,[73] experience. Indeed, his text[74] indicates that he probably operated a sideline as a nurseryman and seedsman, as it states that he has for sale 'garden fruits, rootes and seeds ... at a reasonable price, and perfect good without deceit', and even lists some prices. 'When you propose to sow your garden', he wrote, 'some few days before let it be clean pared and the weeds carried to some convenient place in the garden to rot. ... then dig the garden very small, and as you dig it pick out the roots of weeds as clean as you can and rake it well ... and when all the parings and weedings all the whole year is well rotten then it will be very fine and good earth ... and is very good to rancker the garden in want of other muck.' Both Gardiner, and his pioneering work, deserve to be much better known than they are.

Plate 7: Hoards Park, Bridgnorth,
the main door from the orchard to the house.
The wall is elaborately topped with dog tooth brickwork
and sandstone crests.

*Plate 8: The gatehouse at Upton Cressett,
one of the very first brick houses in the county.*

*Plate 9: Loton deer park, the lodge.
Since this photograph was taken the lodge
has been repaired and rendered, emphasising the
quoining and other architectural details*

Plate 10: Golding Hall, Cound. The later 17th-century terraced garden.

Plate 11: Blodwell Hall, Llanyblodwell. The pediment of the summerhouse of 1718, carved with the marital arms of Lady Ursula Bridgeman. The pediment was originally topped with the family crest, a demi-lion rampant argent, holding between the paws a wreath of laurel proper.

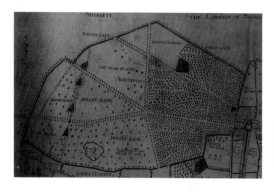

Plate 12: Aldenham, 1722. The great double avenue can be seen approaching the house on the right. The deer park has been cut through with rides and avenues, making it an extension of the pleasure grounds.

Plate 13: At Linley Hall, near More, the grounds were improved in the mid 18th century by Robert More. More, a Fellow of the Royal Society and a friend and pupil of Linnaeus, was a noted botanist, and is credited with having introduced the larch to England.

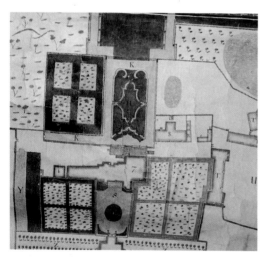

Plate 14: Dothill, Wellington, in 1734. Seen here are the gardens around the house, showing the main axis through the elaborate scrolled parterre and the bowling green with its gravel walks to the end of the long canal.

Plate 15: The Tong estate, 1759. Avenues radiate across the landscape from Tong Castle. The wilderness at the end of the lake can clearly be seen.

The Age of Formality: 1660-1750

Over the course of the mid 17th century radical new French and Dutch ideas about garden design started to enter England, and the work of continental designers such as the Frenchmen André Le Notre, Claude Mollet and his son André was immensely influential. Charles II, first cousin of Louis XIV of France, saw many of the new European gardens first-hand, and within weeks of regaining the kingdom in 1660 had begun to lay out St. James's Park in London. It was in the style of Claude Mollet, one of whose favourite devices was the 'patte d'oie', or goose foot, that is a number of avenues radiating out from a semi-circle like the webbed foot of a bird. Dutch garden styles popularized at this time were also formal and symmetrical, but were more intimate in scale and made much use of 'canals', shallow rectangular ponds, usually set about with clipped evergreens, lead statuary, and flowering bulbs and shrubs.

In Shropshire, as almost everywhere else in Europe, gardens of this era have been almost entirely swept away, usually in the later 18th century when fashions in landscape design swung markedly to favour the informal. Nevertheless, led by the documentary and pictorial evidence, it is possible to see at least something of those lost formal landscapes.

One of the county's finest Dutch gardens may well have been that at Longnor, near Dorrington, where about 1668 Sir Richard Corbett, a wealthy member of county society, began work on a new and fashionable seven-bay brick house. Hand-in-hand with its construction went the laying out of new gardens, shown in paintings of 1670.[1] In front of the house was a gated forecourt with circular pond, apparently containing a statue or fountain, running back from which were four canals with evergreens around their edges. Behind the house were raised walks and summerhouses, while to one side was a cascade which, if the date of about 1668 can be believed, is a remarkably early English example of a 'water staircase'; the celebrated example at West Wycombe (Bucks.) which it resembles was begun by the Dashwoods only after 1710. Here, more than anything, is proof positive of the quality of the lost gardens of Longnor.

The continental fashions in garden design did not meet with unalloyed approval, or understanding.[2] In 1705 the 'Jacobitical, musical, mad Welsh parson' George Llywelyn, friend of Purcell and sometime Page of the Backstairs to Charles II, took the vicarage of Condover and proceeded to rebuild the rectory house and to create a new garden there. Dr. Charles Burney, a contemporary, noted that:

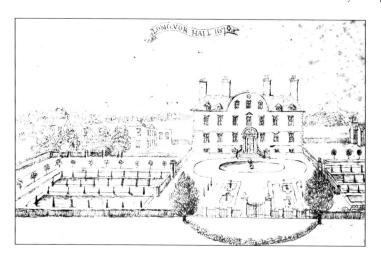

Fig. 16:
Longnor Hall, Dorrington.
Mid 19th-century copies by
Frances Stackhouse Acton of lost
paintings of 1670. They show the newly
completed house and its Dutch garden,
with canals to the front of the house and
a cascade near the walk to the church.

'His house was fitted up with great taste, and had many good pictures in it. But he seems to have spent more time in horticulture than in any other amusement; yet in this, notwithstanding his antipathy to King William, his taste was so peculiarly Dutch, that he cherished "the mournful family of yews" to a risible degree: having at each angle of his parterre, trees of that species cut into the shape of almost every bird and beast that had been preserved in Noah's ark; with satan, the prince of devils, in the centre, for which it was said by the country people he had been offered £1,000; and in a flower bed, just under his parlour window, King David playing on a harp, was cut in box.'

Employment of topiary in this extreme form can also be seen in a painting of Condover Hall,[3] probably executed between about 1710 and 1720. The elaborate evergreen 'cones, globes and pyramids' all appear mature, suggesting that they cannot have been planted much after 1700. This would accord with what is known from elsewhere in the country, in Oxford for instance, where topiary was absent from college gardens in 1675 but prolific and mature in 1733. By the latter date, in fact, polite opinion was turning away from this most elaborate of formal fashions, and already in 1712 Joseph Addison was writing in the *Spectator*:[4]

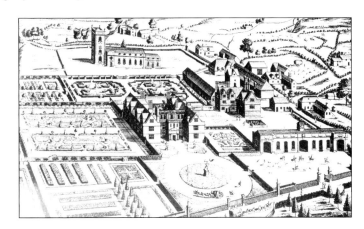

Fig. 17:
Henry Beighton's 1726 prospect
of Castle Bromwich Hall.
The Bridgemans' gardens at Blodwell Hall
were probably very similar.

'Our trees rise in Cones, Globes, and Pyramids. We see the Marks of the Scissars upon every Plant and Bush. I do not know whether I am singular in my Opinion, but, for my own part, I would rather look upon a tree in all its Luxurancy and Diffusion of Boughs and Branches, than when it is thus cut trimmed into a Mathematical Figure.'

Both Condover gardens, Hall and Rectory, like so many formal landscapes, were swept away in the later 18th or early 19th century. One rare survival is the remarkable terraced and sunken garden at Golding Hall, near Cound.[5] This was probably created in the later 17th century by Thomas Langley (d. 1694), a Shrewsbury barrister, who in the 1660s added a brick range on to his father's timber-framed house. Behind are two brick-walled terraces, the upper some five metres high and the lower three metres, both now supported by broad raking buttresses. At one end of the upper terrace, and overlooking the garden, are the foundations of what may be the summerhouse with seven cane chairs mentioned in Langley's will. The terraces resemble, in a modest fashion, those of Powys Castle and, as there, the particular microclimate of the terraces may have been used to grow fruit and vegetables as well as more ornamental items such as topiaried yews. Ornamental evergreens may also have been placed around the earth terraces which ran off the ends of the brick terraces and across the end of the garden. Together the terraces enclosed a flat plat some 30 metres square, today lawn but presumably once a formal parterre.

During the 1980s the gardens created at Castle Bromwich in the 1720s by Sir John Bridgeman were carefully restored, allowing us to see once more what a large and fashionable garden of the early 18th century would have looked like. Bridgeman moved there in 1720 on the death of his wife Ursula, for the previous twenty years their main home having been Blodwell Hall, in Llanyblodwell.[6] Here, too, they had made a great garden. While in many respects Blodwell was apparently a typical garden in the later 17th-century style with lead and stone statuary and a prospect mound giving views both of garden and landscape beyond, the Bridgemans added to it in 1718 a very sophisticated summerhouse in the Classical style, its pediment elaborately carved with their marital arms. Year after year, and from a wide variety of sources including the gardens at Chirk and Halston, plants were introduced: yew (including a 'silver edged' variety), fir, spruce, laurel (some budded on to cherry stocks), mulberry, savin and mezerion trees; striped and silver hollies; striped phillyrea; roses and woodbines. The fruit garden was planted with walnut, pear, peach, apricot and apple trees, sweet briars and gooseberry bushes, while at various times the vegetable garden was supplied with Russian cabbages, cauliflowers, 'Hotspar' peas, carrots and turnips.

Fig. 18:
An 18th-century view of Davenport House,
near Worfield. Francis Smith of Warwick built
the house for Henry Davenport in 1726,
and the avenues were probably planted then.
About 1753 the grounds were improved
with the assistance of William Shenstone,
whose landscape at the Leasowes, Halesowen,
was so influential.

After Sir John's death in 1747 Blodwell Hall was let out as a farmhouse, and the gardens became neglected. Little now survives of them apart from the summerhouse, happily soon to be the subject of a major restoration programme.

Only a few years before the Bridgemans began work at Blodwell the Newports were improving their gardens at Eyton on Severn. Accounts of the 1690s[7] record the firing of bricks for walls associated with the 'best' and kitchen gardens, gravel for the walks arriving by barge, the building of steps up to the mount walk, and the planting of hollies, as well as more routine operations such as making and refinishing stone rollers. Also of about the same date may be the extensive formal gardens shown by air photography to have adjoined Boreatton Hall, built about 1700 for the Hunts.[8]

The great gated forecourt of Blodwell Hall was approached by a 1.5 km long tree-lined walk or avenue paved with spar. This too was probably planted about 1700 as although avenues were not unknown in the 16th century it was only in the later 17th century that they became fashionable - indeed, almost ubiquitous.[9] Such an emphatic demonstration of lordship was found on many other estates, such as Kinlet, Walcot and Aldenham, while at Oakly, near Bromfield, the number of avenues grew from two in 1733[10] to about eight in the 1770s,[11] radiating irregularly across all parts of the park. Most avenues were of lime or elm, although at Linley, near Bishop's Castle, it was beech and oak. A tree ring count suggests that the beech were planted in the 1720s.[12] Another popular tree at this time was the sweet chestnut, used in the later 17th century to form an avenue to Sir Francis

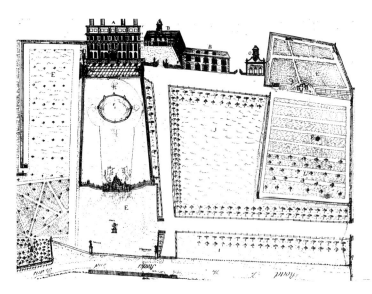

Fig. 19:
Thomas Powis's house and grounds
at Berwick, near Shrewsbury, in 1760,
thirty years after their completion.
In front of the house is a forecourt with
circular 'canal', separated from the outer
court by the Davies brothers great iron
gates. To the left of the courts, running
down to the River Severn (not shown)
are gardens and the wilderness. To the
right, beyond the stables and dove house
is the kitchen garden, with hot house and
greenhouse. Various seats or bowers are
dotted around the grounds, including,
against the left side of the house,
a 'yew arbour'.

Newport's great house at Eyton on Severn, and in the early 18th century to line a drive to The Lodge, at Overton.[13] Once conifers became common they too were used in a similar fashion, as in the mid 19th-century Ladies', or Cedar Walk at Acton Reynald.[14] At much the same time walnuts were used for a half-mile avenue at Eyton upon the Weald Moors. A similar device to the avenue was the ride, cut straight through woodland and usually aligned with the house, as seen on a 1765 plan of Halston and there perhaps dating from the 1690s when the house was rebuilt.[15]

Avenues and rides were usually viewed from the house through an elaborate iron screen or gate in the perimeter wall, which provided further opportunity for statements of power and lineage in the form of crests and armorial overthrows. After these became popular in the later 17th century a number of gatesmiths gained wide renown, among them the Davies brothers of Wrexham who in the 1720s supplied gates for Hawkstone,[16] Berwick (now moved to Newnham Paddox, Warws.) and perhaps Aldenham.[17] The movement of gates and screens, whether within a landscape or, often by sale, to an entirely new property, was (and is) far from uncommon; as well as cases of such features leaving the county instances can be cited of them being brought in, as at Henley Hall, in Bitterley, where the gates and screens came from Wirksworth in Derbyshire.[18]

Another of Shropshire's great 18th-century gardens was Dothill, where the existing small formal landscape, set around the canalized moat of the medieval house, was hugely extended during the first quarter of the century.[19] Unfortunately the architect of the scheme is unknown; whoever, he was fully conversant with the latest design ideas and created an extensive yet integrated landscape incorporating these. By 1734 some seven hectares of formal grounds had been laid out around the house, the main axis leading from the house, through an elaborate parterre, via a bowling green surrounded by gravel walks with summerhouses at their ends, to a long canal. That canal, with a raised terrace down either side, formed one end of a great pool, a view down the length of which could be enjoyed from a grassed amphitheatre which ran down to the water's edge, a feature borrowed from French gardens in the early 18th century by the landscape architect Charles Bridgeman (d. 1738), the key figure in the transition from the rigidly formal gardens of the later 17th and early 18th centuries to the freer designs of William Kent and Capability Brown. To one side of the pool, the left as viewed from the amphitheatre and on a slight hillock, was a 'wood with vistas' - alleys or rides radiating through it from a central clearing to give views of neighbouring houses, churches, and the Wrekin, while on the right-hand side was another wooded feature,

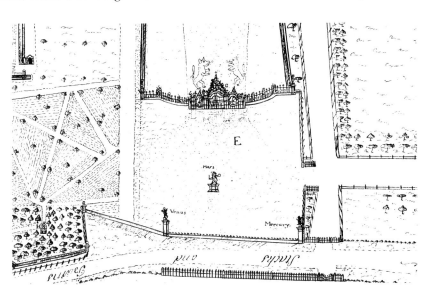

Fig. 20:
The outer court at Berwick in 1760, showing the lead statuary. They were probably painted to resemble stone or bronze, or even naturalistically.

'The Mount with Firs'. Sadly, Dothill House was demolished about 1960, and other than the pool, which survives much as when mapped in 1734, the entire garden has been destroyed and partly built over by houses.

A feature such as the Mount, often called a 'wilderness', and comprising an area of woodland cut through with paths, was typical of larger gardens in the later 17th and early 18th centuries. Here the visitor could experience the sensation of being lost (although comforted by the knowledge that the outside world was never far away), unlike along an avenue or ride where the house would remain, if distantly, always in sight. In the early 18th century at Tong there was a typical wilderness with straight *allées*, swept away along with the formal avenues in the later 1760s when the estate changed hands.[20] Other wildernesses are known to have existed at Kinlet,[21] Berwick House (near Shrewsbury)[22] and Hawkstone.[23] One may also have lain next to the manor at Wem. About 1750 Samuel Garbet reported that its site adjoined fields called the Alleys which had their name from 'the alleys or walks formerly made in them.'[24]

Hawkstone provides an interesting example of how haphazard garden creation could be at this time, proceeding with apparently only the barest overall concept of what was to be done.[25] Its owner was the Hon. and Revd. Richard Hill, who in the 1690s had been Deputy Paymaster to the forces of William III in Flanders, thereby amassing a large fortune by what one friend called 'lucrative arithmetick'. After he retired from public life in 1708 he began to take a more active role in the running of the estate and in the improvement of the Hall, which was refronted at this time, and its gardens. Letters between Hill and his local agents in the early 1720s show the work proceeding slowly, if erratically. Part of the problem clearly was that there was apparently no overall plan. The design, both in general and of specific features, evolved through correspondence and discussion between Hill - who in fact never once visited Hawkstone while the work was going on, preferring to remain at his house in Richmond[26] - his agent, his mason, and even the workmen, who on more than one occasion had to be rebuked for their 'wild notions'[27] and for failing to carry out directions. In 1723, for instance, it was Francis Chambre, the agent, who was 'viewing and setting out' a 'long walk or vista of trees', the Western Avenue, in front of the house. If that was straightforward the laying out in 1725 of another avenue, the 20-foot wide 'fir walk', was less so. There was a good deal of debate both about its line - to keep it straight would involve filling in an eight-foot deep pond, and Chambre favoured carrying it round the pond to save money and because 'its turning will be pleasant and amusing'[28] - and whether to use spruce or the cheaper Scots pine.[29] Next to the Hall the main feature was a great 290-yard long parterre court, cut through with diagonal paths rather in the manner of a wilderness. Beyond lay other features, such as the 'dunge' or wilderness, for which seats were made and painted in 1725 although Chambre was very angry because they had not been done to the agreed design.[30] Within or next to the wildernes was 'the Rock'; lying only 100 yards from one of the main courts around the house[31] this was a prominent feature, and there was a good deal of debate about what could be done with it. In September 1726 Chambre had a site meeting at the Rock with William Price, the mason, at which they considered instructions sent by their master and also 'directions' by the celebrated gardener Sir Thomas Hanmer (d. 1678) of Bettisfield, the latter presumably in the form of a manuscript supplied by Hill. Once the plan was clear the mason's men 'immediately fell to the work in getting stone and cutting the rock for the cave.'[32] Within four months the work was complete and the Rock had a noble look, 'the beauty of which would be seen a great way.'[33] Hill had had the idea of having this cave excavated for some time, but it is interesting, and again indicative of how open the process of design was, that three months earlier Price had felt able to suggest an alternative scheme whereby the Rock was surmounted by a summerhouse, 'which would make a pleasanter walk from the house.' Hill thanked him for 'his thoughts concerning my awkward rock', but resolved for the moment to do nothing.[34] By that time work on the gardens was drawing to a close, indicated by the purchase in 1725 of wrought iron gates for the middle court from Robert Davies of Wrexham, one of the best known gatesmiths of the age.[35]

The use of Scots pine and possibly spruce at Hawkstone is a good example of the increased availability in the early 18th century of coniferous species. Often, as there, the newly available trees and shrubs were set out in formal, linear arrangements, of the type which had become widespread over the previous two or three generations. Occasionally, however, some of the new ideas propounded by Stephen Switzer, Batty Langley, Charles Bridgeman and William Kent, all broadly favouring a softer, supposedly more 'natural' style, were adopted, as at Linley, near Bishop's Castle. Here, about 1750,[36] at the same time that the house was rebuilt, Robert More - traveller, botanist and friend of Linnaeus - planted some of the earliest larch to be grown in England, not in avenues but in a scenic grouping in a sheltered valley.[37] The larch soon became widely available and popular, and specimens were reputedly planted in the garden of Shrewsbury's Whitehall at much the same time as More was planting them at Linley.[38]

Reconstruction of house and garden often followed the acquisition or inheritance of a property by a new owner. When Edward Fleming (reputedly an unpleasant man, ultimately to be poisoned with arsenic) bought the Sibdon Castle estate from his father in 1744 his thoughts immediately turned to lake digging and the planting of avenues.[39] The same process also occurred at Hardwick Hall, near Ellesmere, where a splendid new house, possibly by Francis Smith of Warwick, was built about 1720 for John Kynaston who had bought the estate in 1693 (Plate 16). Elaborate wrought iron gates, now sold, probably led into the forecourt, off which a damp, linear depression suggests the presence of a canal, carrying the eye down the main axis from the house.[40] A very similar arrangement of canal and gates was installed at much the same time at Moor Park, near Ludlow. Here the house was rebuilt and new gardens laid out after it was inherited in 1715 by Richard Salwey, whose grandfather of the same name had been an M.P. and Cromwell's ambassador to Constantinople.

Fig. 21:
Van Nost's statue of Hercules,
originally at Condover Hall.
When moved to the Quarry it was
placed with its back to the town,
in order to reduce the offence
the 'brawny god' gave to
the ladies of the town.

To commemorate their completion Salwey commissioned a painting of Moor Park by Vogelsanck and Lens (Plate 17), which shows the main feature of the gated forecourt to have been a pair of lead statues of classical figures. Lead work was often painted to resemble more expensive materials such as marble, bronze, or stone, or even in polychrome to give figures a more life-like effect. It may be that a parterre designed by George London (d. 1714) on the far side of the house (see Frontispiece) was retained when the house was built.

Such statues, along with lead vases, had become highly fashionable in England about 1680.
By about 1700 a statue of Mercury stood in the centre of an elaborate garden in Dogpole, Shrewsbury, while about 1718 £19 10s. was paid for 'two lead figures and two stone figures together with the cases and carriage' for the new gardens at Blodwell. At Berwick in 1760 the outer court was dominated by three statues, of Mercury, Mars, and Venus. One of the most highly regarded sculptors producing statuary was John Van Nost (d.1729), who had a workshop near Green Park, London. Several examples of his work survive in Shropshire, even if not in their original setting, as well as at Powys Castle in Montgomeryshire. At Aldenham, where there was apparently a major re-ordering of the landscape in the early 18th century, a statue of Neptune is attributed to Van Nost, as is one of Hercules which was originally the centrepiece of the entrance court at Condover Hall but which since 1851 has stood in the Quarry, in Shrewsbury.

Increasingly urban gardens, too, seem to have been set out for pleasure. When Celia Fiennes visited Whitchurch in 1698 two gardens took her notice:

> 'One belongs to an apothecary full of all fruits and greens, the other was at
> the Crown Inn where I stayed, it was exceedingly neat with orange and lemon
> trees, myrtle, striped and gilded holly trees, box and filleroy [phillyrea] finely
> cut and firs and Merumsuracum [Marum Syriacum] which makes the fine
> snuff, and fine flowers, all things almost in a little tract of garden ground.'[41]

The appearance of a fashionable town garden at this time is shown in a fine painting of about 1700 of a garden in Dogpole, Shrewsbury (Plates 18-19). It is surrounded by tall brick walls, with summerhouses at the end corners between which are placed urns containing evergreens,

Fig. 22:
The summerhouse built about 1730 by
Dr. Phillips at 12 St. John's Hill, Shrewsbury.

Plate 16: Hardwick Hall, Ellesmere.
There was originally a linear canal, like that at Moor Park,
leading off from the court in front of the house.

*Plate 17: Moor Park, Ludlow. A view of 1722 by Vogelsanck and Lens
commissioned to mark the house's completion. The new gardens
included espalier fruit, lead statues, and a canal (bottom centre).
The canvas was later re-used and the house over-painted
with a favourite bitch.*

*Plate 18: A fashionable private garden in Dogpole, Shrewsbury,
about 1700. The painting is dominated by the garden,
and may therefore be a record of a recently completed project.
The intricacy of the design suggests a professional hand.*

*Plate 19: In this detail the owners, or their guests, are shown on the gravel walks,
which a gardener is rolling. The treatment of the borders along the edges of the walks
is typical of the time, with flowers such as hyacinths, tulips, snapdragons
and chrysanthemums between clipped yews.*

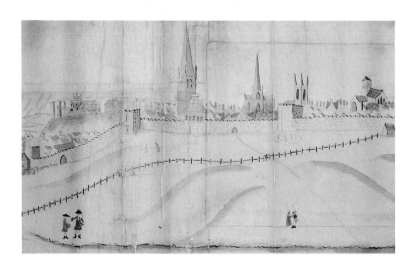

Plate 20: The Quarry, Shrewsbury, about 1700,
before the lime avenues were planted. As can be seen,
the riverside walk was already fashionable.

Fig. 23:
An early 18th-century summerhouse
off Quarry Place, Shrewsbury.

busts of classical figures, and a square sundial with a gnomon on every face. Also from the world of antiquity is the lead figure of Mercury in the centre of the garden, the turf of which is cut into symmetrical and typically English parterres, edged with flower borders and bounded by gravel paths. Spaced around the garden are numerous clipped 'greens' - that is evergreens - such as Celia Fiennes saw at Whitchurch. This was not the only fashionable garden in the street, and in 1695 it was said that the Earl of Bradford's house, later to become the Guildhall, was among several which had 'hanging gardens' descending down the slope to the River Severn.[42] Scrub clearance in 1996 revealed the terraces of what are probably elements of these gardens, dropping down in four or five flights from the town walls to the river.

Summerhouses seem to have been springing up all over towns at this time, perhaps the clearest indication of all that even modest gardens were becoming pleasure grounds. In Shrewsbury several, like those at the end of the Dogpole garden, were built along the line of the town walls. In 1686 the Corporation granted William Corbett a plot 'for his Somer house on the Town Wall near St. Mary's',[43] while photographs show that until demolished in the mid 20th century there was a tower-like summerhouse with mullioned and transomed windows at the top of the north side of Wyle Cop.[44] Others were built in and around the fashionable St. John's Hill area. About 1730 the Revd. Dr. Phillips, the headmaster of Shrewsbury School, had what has been described as

Fig. 24:
The Quarry, Shrewsbury,
as shown on a plan of 1746.
The summerhouse in fig. 23
is the upper of the two at the ends
of the garden encroaching
into the Quarry (top right,
left of the bowling green).

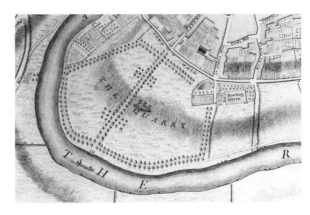

Fig. 25: The Bucks' 1732 view of the Quarry from Kingsland.
Townspeople of the better sort can be seen along the riverside walk.

a 'country house in minature'[45] built at 12 St. John's Hill. In the back garden stood a two-storey octagonal summerhouse containing a finely panelled upper room with fireplace, suitable for dining in. At much the same time a pair of smaller, but still architecturally elaborate summerhouses, was erected at 5 Quarry Place, overlooking the new Quarry walks. Although the function of such buildings probably varied from season to season, and according to whether it was the family, or male, or female company which was gathered there, Thomas Pennant was confident in his description of their principal use, at least in north Wales. His father's house, for instance, was 'attended with (what was very frequent in the Principality) a summer house, at a very small distance, and a cellar beneath, used as retreat for jolly owners and their friends to enjoy, remote from the fair, their toasts and noisy meriment.'[46]

The Quarry walks, lined with avenues of limes, were laid out in 1719 at the mayor's expense on the town's common grazing land, land which had long been dug in to for stone and clay.[47] By that time 'the walk by the Severn side' had already been fashionable for a number of years,[48] and in 1705 the Irish dramatist George Farquhar set a scene of his *Recruiting Officer* there. Walks, like assembly rooms, were places for the quality to meet, to exchange news, and simply to be seen. When John Byng visited Shrewsbury in 1793 he recorded how his host, Mr. M., while in the Quarry walks, 'had to bow to everyone, and then to relate their histories to us.'

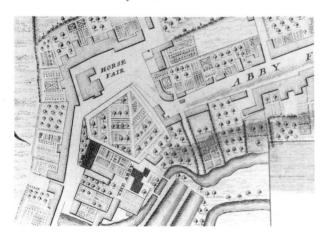

Fig. 26:
Shrewsbury's Abbey Gardens,
described in 1698 by Celia Fiennes,
occupied the area between Shrewsbury Abbey
and Horse Fair. Although apparently no
longer open in 1746 their layout can still
be seen on John Rocque's town plan.

The success of the Quarry and the growing fashionability of the town led to the creation of other public facilities for the well-to-do, alongside more private and commercial speculations such as coffee houses, bowling greens, horse races, and about 1760 a theatre. In 1728 the Corporation established an exclusive 'airing' for the 'gentry' across the river from the Quarry in Kingsland, a place, as in some London parks, where select people were allowed to ride on horseback or in their carriages. They paid an annual subscription to the Corporation, and in return were furnished with a key to the gates. It was presumably to improve the setting that trees were being moved about there in 1737 under the direction of the mayor and others, while in 1742 when the Corporation leased out Kingsland the right was reserved 'for Gentlemen and Ladies to air their coaches and horseback'.

Also in the earlier 18th century, Angus McInnes argues, another set of walks became fashionable, this time around the town walls, which gave distant views across the Shropshire countryside. Richard Pococke, visiting the town in 1736, thought the prospect from the castle area 'one of the finest views I ever saw', sufficient to make Shrewsbury 'the Paradise of England' and a rival to Lyon, Arles, Avignon and the towns of Flanders. Pennant, writing in the 1770s, also mentions the wall walks, but whether in fact anything was done to the walls in the 18th century to facilitate their perambulation remains unknown.

The Quarry walks were not, in fact, the county's first. The Castle Walk around the hill top at Bridgnorth was said in 1739 to be about 590 yards long, 'a very pleasant and healthful walk ... curiously set with elms.' By then it was well established, and locally it was believed that it had been much admired by Charles I during the Civil War.[49] At Oswestry[50] the Broad Walk, alongside the churchyard, was planted with trees by the Revd. Thomas Owen, vicar 1707-13. Gate pillars were erected at the entrance to the walk soon after, and in 1738 the parish commissioned fine wrought iron gates from John and Robert Davies, the celebrated Welsh gatesmiths. By the end of the century an alcove or summerhouse had been erected at the far end of the walk, although in the early 19th century when it was the resort of 'questionable characters' there were proposals that it should be pulled down, which it finally was in 1854. Earlier still were Shrewsbury's Abbey Gardens, which much impresssed Celia Fiennes when she visited the town in 1698. These probably lay east of the Abbey church, an area known historically as the 'gaia' or 'gay', a name given to small parks or ornamental enclosures. At the Abbey Gardens there were 'gravel walks set full of all sorts of greens, orange and lemon trees ... there was also firs, myrtles and hollies of all sorts and a greenhouse full of all sorts of curiosities of flowers and greens, there was the aloes plant. Out of this went another garden, much larger and with several fine walks kept exactly cut and rolled for the company to walk in; every Wednesday most of the town, the ladies and gentlemen walk there as in St. James's Park ...'[51]

Sadly no trace of these remarkable grounds survives. The greenhouse is one of the first known in Shropshire and is a very early example of this type of building, a type somewhat different from its modern namesake. Usually single storey, with a well glazed front wall and artificially heated using stoves and flues, it was to such buildings that the newly introduced 'tender greens' - that is evergreens such as orange and lemon trees - would be transferred in their pots once frosts threatened. Other, broadly synonymous, terms for such buildings were 'conservatory' (because they conserved the expensive plants) and 'orangery', which emphasises the popularity of the orange tree, introduced to England in 1590. Perhaps the earliest such building in Shropshire was at the Newport's mansion at Eyton on Severn, where in 1688 Alice Bottfield was paid a shilling a week for helping in the 'glasshouse'.[52] Summerhouses, too, such as that of 1718 at Blodwell,[53] may sometimes have been designed to have doubled as orangeries. At Hardwick the death of Edward Kynaston precipitated a sale in 1775, the contents of which included 'a great quantity of very large, valuable

Fig. 27:
The orangery at Pitchford, photographed in the 1940s. The roof was probably a Victorian replacement, but otherwise the building was much as built in the 18th century.

and healthy orange and lemon trees and a variety of greenhouse plants'.[54] Old fashioned by this date they apparently failed to find a buyer as two years later the *Shrewsbury Chronicle* carried a further advertisement offering for sale at Hardwick '14 orange trees in tubs, full of fruit, and in a most healthy condition.'[55] A rare survival is the fine glazed orangery at Pitchford, probably of the late 18th century, although sadly this was converted into a house some time after the Second World War. At Berwick, north of Shrewsbury, the kitchen garden in 1760 contained not only a greenhouse but also a hothouse, both perhaps built in the 1730s (Fig. 19). In hothouses, first mentioned in the 1660s, dung and heated walls were used to grow succulent fruits and vegetables such as vines, apricots, melons and cucumbers. Such developments, which brought prestigious and exotic produce to the table, greatly boosted the importance of the kitchen garden, and of the gardener who oversaw it.

Having said that, little is known about these men, some of whom at least were well educated in their profession not only as a result of practical experience but also from reading; the listed subscribers to Stephen Switzer's short-lived monthly periodical *The Practical Husbandman and Gardener* which ran between 1733-34 included both John Walcot of Walcot Hall and Thomas Dobbs, his gardener. Walcot's kitchen gardens must at the time have been among the county's best, and detailed accounts of 1703-6 record their construction.[56] The quantities of materials used

GARDENS.

127 Three garden rakes, garden line, sharavel, and mattock
128 Two pruning nippers and garden shears
129 Three garden rakes, daisy ditto, two scuffles, and hoe
130 Three garden rakes, three hedgers, root spade, and small sharavel
131 Two axes, brushing hooks, riddle, &c.
132 Thirteen hand glasses, in lots
133 Thirty twig shades
134 Two trainers and scythe
135 Quantity of netting
136 Four wire flower guards
137 Three watering cans
138 Three ditto
139 About twenty dozen of flower pots
140 One light cucumber frame
141 Two ditto ditto
142 Two ditto melon ditto
143 Three ditto ditto
144 Six cucumber frame lights
145 Garden engine
146 Several dozens of choice greenhouse plants, in pots
147 Capital cast-iron garden roller
148 Bee bench
149 Wall step ladder
150 Sundries, in lots.

END OF SEVENTH DAY'S SALE.

Fig. 28: (far left)
A 1708 engraving of a lemon tree in its portable container.

Fig. 29: (left)
Lots in the garden, from the catalogue for the 1836 sale at Tedsmore Hall, near West Felton, Oswestry.

were enormous. Overall some 700,000 bricks were used (just in 1703 nearly 45,000 faggots being burnt in the brick clamps) and nearly 7,500 horse loads of lime for mortar. Other sums were spent on hundreds of yards of coping stone, 2,700 iron hooks presumably for fruit cordon wires, making wheelbarrows and melon frames, buying and staking trees, and on tools and unspecified expert advice from London. While the gardens were being established hares proved a particular problem, and hedge bottoms had to be stopped with gorse to keep them out.

Most of the tools familiar to modern gardeners were already available. At Benthall Hall in 1720 the garden tools included a stone roller, a ladder (for dealing with the fruit trees), a scythe, shears, a rake, a spade, a hoe, a 'wire riddle' and a watering pan.[57] The last was presumably a metal vessel akin to the modern watering can, whereas at Willey Hall in 1726 they still used watering pots, presumably pottery versions. There, in addition to what the Benthall gardener had, there were iron rakes, bagging bills, knives, a French hoe, three-tine forks and a 'single fork', shears, a ten-foot measuring rod, a garden line, a grafting saw, twelve mats for the hot beds and five 'sinklers', presumably dibbers.[58] Also commonly found in larger gardens by this time, although not listed at either Benthall or Willey, were glass bell jars for protecting tender plants. In 1761 at Park Hall, Oswestry, there were twenty, three for the hot beds and seventeen 'hand glasses' of various sizes.[59] They remained in use well in to the 19th century, and thirteen were among the garden implements at Tedsmore Hall offered for sale in 1836.[60]

Although large and in some respects self sufficient, with seeds and bulbs stored over winter in special stores, such gardens would even so have bought in a good deal of stock from specialist nurseries, especially when 'choice' fruit of the latest improved varieties was sought. Until the early 18th century the number of suppliers in the provinces, men like John Rea of Kinlet, was very limited, but thereafter more and more men entered the trade as both pleasure grounds and kitchen gardens became larger and stocked with ever widening varieties of trees, flowers, fruits and vegetables.

Fig. 30:
The Central Avenue in
Shrewsbury's Quarry in the late 19th century.
Already many of the closely planted limes
were over mature. At the end of the Avenue
Hercules can be seen in the position
to which he was moved in the later
19th century, on the river bank.

In Shropshire Rea's own nursery was carried on after his death in 1677 by his daughter Minerva, whose husband the Revd. Samuel Gilbert in 1683 published *The Florist's Vade Mecum* , which soon established itself as a standard work on the subject.[61] Quite how long the Kinlet nursery survived is unknown, but others soon took its place. Thomas Wright of Bicton, just west of Shrewsbury, furnished some 400 lime trees for the avenues planted in the Quarry in Shrewsbury in 1719,[62] and in 1725 supplied trees for Hawkstone.[63] Four years earlier, in 1721, (when described as of Shelton, which lies on the edge of Bicton township) he had offered to provide variegated hollies for Sir John Bridgeman's garden at Castle Bromwich. Whether or not that tender was accepted he was an intermittent supplier of plants for the garden there for many years, and in 1740 sent fruit trees, ivies and phillyreas ordered by Sir John's son.[64] For the Bridgemans' other great garden, at Blodwell Hall, some plants seem to have been bought from well established gardens. The accounts[65] mention purchases from Mr. Jordan, who was the gardener at Chirk Castle, and from the Halston gardener. Three other major suppliers, Messrs. Langford, Thomas and Howells, the last by far the most important source for plants between 1705 and 1711, for the moment remain unidentified, although Howells at least seems likely to have been a nurseryman.

In the course of the mid and late 17th century florists' societies sprang up in many parts of the country, reflecting this new interest in flowers. Among those sharing that enthusiasm was clearly Bulkley Mackworth, of Buntingsdale Hall, near Market Drayton, whose commonplace jottings for 1710-12 record lists of different types of auricula, carnation, polyanthus, hollyhock, anemone, and ranunculus and where in the garden - in the 'upper quarter next to the house' - he had planted them out [66]. He was also careful to note when potting or planting took place (there was a greenhouse here by 1712), adhering firmly to the belief that the time around the full moon was best, and also his various different potting mixes. Some auriculas, for instance, were sown in mould (humus) mixed with blood and some in 'best mould' mixed with willow mould. One would like to know far more about Mackworth and his garden, and especially whether it was remodelled at about this time to complement the new house built to the design of Francis Smith of Warwick and completed c. 1721.

Many nurserymen seem to have begun as gardeners. Among them can be counted John Whittingham, who established the first, and in the later 18th century most important nursery in the Coventry area. The son of a baker, he was born in Shifnal in 1696 and in 1711 was apprenticed to Samuel Chapman, a Shrewsbury gardener, for a premium of £10.[67] Interestingly, another Whittingham, Thomas, was apprenticed in 1718 to a Wem gardener, Thomas Heath.[68] Professional market gardeners are occasionally identified as such in sources such as the suit list of April 1668, where there are five among the 1,207 male householders in Shrewsbury whose occupation is noted.[69] Far more detailed information is sometimes provided by probate inventories, such as that of William Head of Bridgnorth, who died about 1740.[70] At the time of his death Head had vegetables growing in five different plots of land including his own garden, and their value was appraised by two other Bridgnorth gardeners, James Cureton and William Crapp. His main crop, worth £9, was three-quarters of an acre of potatoes, next in importance being cucumbers (£1 5s.) and onions (£1) with smaller amounts of broccoli, winter greens, red cabbage, French beans, peas and 'sursey', perhaps the parsnipy root vegetable salsify. The main, if not sole produce grown by these men would have been vegetables, cultivated for sale to townsmen. Around several Shropshire towns including Ludlow, Market Drayton, Shifnal and Bridgnorth, at least sections of the complex medieval open fields survived until well into the 19th century,[71] and many of the individual strips were probably given over to vegetable growing. In Bridgnorth the rocky sides of the hill on which the town stands were also largely used for that purpose, and writing in 1739 Richard Cornes recorded that although shallow the hillside soils, when well manured, 'produce great and very early crops of peas, beans, cucumbers, asparagus and all sorts of garden herbs in perfection.'[72]

A Taste for Views and Wind: 1750-1820

In 1747 Arthur Weaver of Morville Hall, north-west of Bridgnorth, was elected M.P.
Weaver obviously felt his 16th-century house unbecoming a man of his new standing, and brought
in the leading architect William Baker to remodel it and bring it up to date.[1] He also embarked upon
a programme of improvements to its grounds in an attempt to make them equally fashionable, quite
possibly acting as his own designer. The results, at least according to Thomas Percy, were not entirely
successful. In a letter of 1760 to William Shenstone, he reported that:

> *'Last year died a Mr. Weaver ... who was possessed by the very demon of*
> *caprice. He came into the possession of an old mansion that commanded a*
> *straight view down a most pleasing vale, and contrived to intercept it by two*
> *straight lines of elms that ran in an oblique direction across it, and which led*
> *the eye to a pyramidal obelisk composed of one single board set up endways by*
> *the joiner of the village. This obelisk, however, was soon removed by the first*
> *puff of wind.*
>
> *In view of one of his windows grew a large, spreading ash, which though the*
> *spontaneous gift of nature was really a fine object, and by its stately figure*
> *and cheerful verdure afforded a most pleasing relief to the eye; you will stare*
> *when I tell you that Mr. W. had this tree painted white, leaves and all. It is*
> *true the leaves soon fell off and the tree died, but the skeleton still remains, as*
> *a monument of its owner's wisdom and ingenuity.'*

What Weaver's efforts were being compared with, although this is not explicitly stated,
was Shenstone's own work on his estate at The Leasowes, Halesowen, then in Shropshire.[2]
Shenstone, poet and landscape theorist - it was apparently he who coined the phrase 'landskip-
gardening' - had only a modest estate but it did include wooded valleys, rushing streams,
the ruins of a priory, and higher ground giving views to the local hills. Here, between 1745 and 1763,
he created a landscape inspired by the Arcadian poets in what became known as the Natural style,
wherein the visitor took a prescribed route to experience a series of vistas with waterfalls, lakes
and pools, bridges, a grotto and modest garden buildings. Latin inscriptions invoking Classical
associations were nailed to seats, trees and alcoves, while at various points there were urns
dedicated to the memory of friends. The whole was variously designed to evoke grandeur,
beauty and in the case of the urns, melancholy.

Fig. 31:
'A View in Virgil's Grove, at the Leasows,
in the County of Salop.' An engraving after
a view by Thomas Smith of Derby showing
tourists enjoying the scenery.

Although The Leasowes did not long survive Shenstone's death, it was for a few years one of the most visited landscape gardens in the country. It and a few other schemes, especially those of William Kent, were so influential that the old ideas of landscape adornment as espoused by Mr. Weaver, with hedges, trees and canals laid out in rigid and formal patterns dominated by straight lines, were very soon abandoned in favour of the new 'natural' style. In the decades which followed many such landscapes were created in the county, a good number of them in place of older, formal layouts. With the natural style came a demand for more and increasingly architecturally varied garden buildings, and by the late 18th century Shropshire had seen a rich flowering of temples, pavilions, seats, bridges and the like in a variety of styles: Classical, gothick, Chinese, Indian, and rustick. Later 18th-century gothick summerhouses by the well-known architect T.F. Pritchard survive behind a house in Broad Street, Ludlow, at Broseley Hall, an eclectic mixture of the styles was combined in the Hermitage, an 'Indian temple' built at Walcot in 1802-3 as a thatched roundhouse surrounded by a verandah. Sadly this was deliberately burnt down in the mid 20th century, presumably to reduce the estate's repair bills. The estate woodman ordered to light the fire recalled thirty years later that 'The floor inside was laid with coloured flag stones. The roof and walls were prettily designed like Chinese wicker work ... It was rather an uncanny place and too beautiful to describe.'[3] Buildings of various types - an artificial ruin , a grotto and cascade, a bamboo

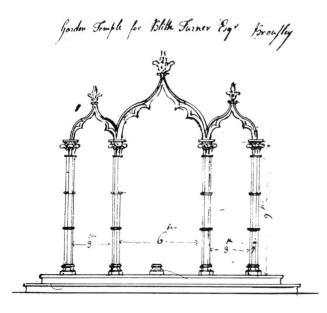

Fig. 32:
Pritchard's design for the facade
of a gothick garden temple
at Broseley Hall.

Plate 21: Millichope Park, Steuart's temple of 1770.

*Plate 22: Sham Castle (also known as Black Dick's Tower)
in Acton Burnell Park, built in 1779-80.*

*Plate 23: The roof of the later 18th-century shell grotto
in Acton Burnell park. Such shellwork was often undertaken
as a hobby by the ladies of the house.*

*Plate 24: Tong Lodge 1840. Few buildings on the Tong estate
seem to have escaped the Durants' improving attentions.*

*Plate 25: An early 19th-century watercolour by Emma Hill,
one of a series of the Hawkstone landscape, apparently entitled
'A distant view of the windmill from Redcastle Hill'.*

*Plate 26: An anonymous early 19th-century watercolour
of another of the Hawkstone tableaux, 'The scene at Otaheite',
reflecting contemporary interest in the lands opened up by
the voyages of discovery to the South Seas.*

Plate 27: Walcot, as mapped in 1827.
The great curving lake was an enlargement of earlier fishponds.

Plate 28: (Above) The Birdhouse.
Lancaster University archaeologists
at work in the Birdhouse, 1994.

Plate 29: (Left) Badger Dingle,
the Rotunda. This seat, and
the Birdhouse, were probably
both designed about 1780
by James Wyatt.

bridge, and a gothick temple - appear in imaginative views by Thomas Robins of the grounds of Davenport House, Worfield, undertaken during the course of improvements by its owner, Sharington Davenport, about 1753-54. Davenport was a friend of Shenstone, and letters suggest the latter advised on the works there.[4]

Shenstone was far from being the only landowner-designer. At Millichope Park in the later 1760s Thomas More, by then an old man, laid out the grounds with memorials to his four sons, all of whom had predeceased him.[5] The main foci were a fine ten-metre high obelisk and a round, Ionic, temple of 1770 designed by George Steuart. The view of the temple from the house was much improved in the mid 19th century when the pool above which it stands was enlarged and a dramatic cliff-top setting created (Plate 21). Another example may be Acton Burnell, where in the later 18th century the Smythes not only rebuilt the Hall but also added a number of adornments to the park including a hilltop octagonal shell grotto, a gothick cottage or lodge, and in 1779-80 a prospect tower called Sham Castle with a triangular plan and circular corner towers (plates 22-23). It was probably also at this time that decorative battlements were added to Acton Burnell Castle. Another possible introduction to the park was a large model of the iron bridge, purchased by Sir Edward Smythe about 1782 from the brother of the designer T.F. Pritchard.[6] The Acton Burnell landscape has many similarities to that created at the same time at Sundorne, near Shrewsbury, where again a military theme was to the fore in the style of the buildings.[7] Those included Haughmond Castle, a lodge or hunting box on top of Haughmond Hill perhaps designed by the architect responsible for improvements at Sundorne Castle, Robert Mylne. Both Acton Burnell and Sundorne had large lakes, the latter described as 'new made' in 1777,[8] and at both the circuit around the landscape was unusually long (reputedly five miles in the case of Sundorne) and with high ground providing a stunning view of the house and its estate. Also common to both was the central part played in the landscape by the gothick ruins, of Acton Burnell Castle and Haughmond Abbey, John Corbet repairing the latter as part of his Sundorne improvements.[9]

Fig. 33:
A late 19th-century
photograph of Haughmond
Castle, showing how it
formed the centrepiece
of a picturesque landscape.

Fig. 34:
The door of the Nursery, the scallop shell
in the tympanum reflecting the Dovaston's
interests in the natural sciences. The house was
demolished and its grounds largely built over
in the 1980s, one of the worst losses in the
county of an historic landscape in recent years.

On a smaller scale is the example of Earlsdale, near Pontesbury. In 1794 this was visited by Richard Hodgkinson, a Lancashire gentleman and journal keeper. He noted how its owner, Richard Heighway, had returned to the country after several years in London with an intention to settle. 'He fixed upon a situation, almost as romantic as imagination can conceive and has built a new house upon it. A little above his house is a most beautiful waterfall, issuing out of a large wood, which covers a high hill behind his house. In front of his house is a very high and barren mountain, the upper part of which is very steep and rocky ... His garden which lies at the front of the house is extensive and laid out with great taste; the walks, the water and the plantations are beautiful but everything here is in its infancy, in a few years this promises to be a very sweet place. The garden has no cultivation but from Mr. Heighway's own hand. He digs, plants, sows and prunes and when he is tired with this, he goes into the house and amuses himself with portrait painting in which he is a very capital artist.'[10] Also of modest scale were the grounds of The Nursery, at West Felton near Oswestry, laid out by the polymathic father and son John (d. 1808) and J.F.M. (d. 1854) Dovaston. In the later 19th century the grounds were said to contain trees representative of every country in the world, these including the celebrated Dovaston, or Weeping, Yew, said to have been planted in 1777 and the country's oldest surviving specimen.[11] Those stood among various architectural antiquities and the younger Dovaston's rock collection. In 1829, following a quarrel with the village parson, he formed nine of the larger geological specimens into a cromlech or pseudo-prehistoric tomb which he intended as his burial place, although by the time of his death he was reconciled to the church.[12]

A bamboo bridge at Davenport was part of a craze for Chinese houses and motifs - chinoiserie as it is known - which spread rapidly across England from the 1730s, and which enjoyed such popularity that in the 1750s Horace Walpole was drawn to complain at the number of Chinese buildings which

Fig. 35:
The mid 18th-century chinoiserie
summerhouse at Orleton.
The oriental embellishments are to
a garden building of traditional design
(see for instance Fig. 22), with a service
basement below a principal room
approached via a flight of stairs.

abounded.[13] Shropshire probably had its fair share, although few have survived because most were usually built largely of softwood. The Chinese temple at Hawkstone disappeared between 1832 and 1850, only slightly outlasting the nearby Egyptian Tent.[14] A lattice-fronted pagoda built by the Topp family at Whitton Hall survived much longer but was in such poor condition in 1985 that it had to be entirely dismantled,[15] while chinoiserie bridges at places such as Millichope have been replaced many times. As far as is known the only substantial building of this type to survive largely intact is a splendid summerhouse at Orleton, just outside Wellington, probably built for the Cluddes in the mid 18th century.

It was apparently in the 1740s that Sir Rowland Hill began to landscape and adorn the craggy sandstone hills, one already surmounted with a ruined 13th-century castle, which adjoined Hawkstone Hall.[16] The first indication of this comes in a description of the ornamental walks written in 1748 by Philip Yorke,[17] who observed:

> *'The place has great rude [i.e. wild] beauties and the owner is continually*
> *improving it. The rocks are more frequent and wild than those at Studley*
> *[Royal] and the prospect more extensive and various ... There is a vineyard,*
> *hot house and kitchen garden laid out on the side of the hill, a most warm spot.*
> *Great part of the walling is cut out of the natural rock, and in the midst of it*
> *is a Gothic turret with battlements ... The terrace runs along about 3/4 mile*
> *on the top of the hill, and looks down into a winding valley, which opens at*
> *once into a fine view of the country, as far as the Shropshire Wrekin and the*
> *Denbighshire hills ...'*

Fig. 36:
Hawkstone: Grotto Rock and Red Castle,
as seen across Hawk Lake, in an engraving
of 1804. By the early 19th century boating
had become an essential element of the
Hawkstone experience.

Fig. 37:
Visitors admire the cavernous grotto at
Hawkstone, under construction in 1765.
It is reached via a pitch black, rock-cut tunnel
sixty metres long, which greatly amplifies
the Stygian atmosphere. By way of deliberate
contrast the exit gives directly on to a cliff top
terrace, with precipitous drops all round.

Over the next half century this became one of the most celebrated sublime landscapes in Europe, with visitors encountering a series of contrasting experiences, one moment groping down pitch dark tunnels and the next facing precipitous cliffs with dizzying vistas beyond (Plates 25-26). In 1774 Dr. Johnson recalled 'its prospects, the awfulness of its shades, the horrors of its precipices, the verdure of its hollows and the loftiness of its rocks ... above is inaccessible altitude, below is horrible profundity.' For the modern scholar the great frustration is that when and by whom the various towers, seats, bridges and other features set around the walks were conceived is largely unknown, as is how much should be attributed directly to Sir Rowland (d. 1783) and especially Sir Richard Hill (d. 1809), his son and heir. Certainly the role of the latter, an enthusiastic Calvanistic Methodist and philanthropist, in opening up and enhancing Hawkstone was important. Two editions of a guide or *Description* were published within a year of him inheriting the estate, and an inn for visitors was opened at much the same time. By then the features included a grotto; 'a rustic sofa covered in moss'; a 'hermit's summer residence' (complete with hermit); a menagerie with eagle, parrots and monkeys; buildings including a summerhouse and cold bath, the White Tower (its inside walls adorned with frescoes of the four seasons) and the Greenhouse; and various natural features with names such as the Ravens' Shelf, Paoli's Point, and the Awful Precipice. Further attractions including lakes, a new entrance at a building called Neptune's Whim, and the 100-foot high Monument were added over the next decade or so, while the grotto, a cavernous room supported on rock columns, was encrusted with 'costly shells, selected from the remotest regions of the sea, and inlaid with petrifactions and fossils from the deepest recesses of the earth.' Although, understandably, it went unmentioned, those 'petrifactions' included a good deal of Coalbrookdale slag!

After many decades of neglect a major programme of restoration was undertaken at Hawkstone in 1992-3, and although many of the features described in the 18th and 19th century guides are now lost it is again possible for the visitor to experience the sensations and views which gained it such fame. Once more Hawkstone is becoming a major attraction for the discerning tourist.

Increasingly, from the mid 18th century, landowners brought in professional designers to create or improve landscapes, and some achieved considerable renown. Best known, then as now, was Lancelot Brown, usually called 'Capability' because of his habit of telling a client when viewing his estate 'There are great capabilities here' - in other words it was capable of improvement. In all, between the late 1740s and his death in 1783, he executed over 170 major commissions, and a wag reputedly joked that he hoped he died before Brown in order to see Heaven before it, too, was improved.[18] It has been estimated that at the height of his career in the 1760s and early 1770s his practice was regularly turning over £15,000, a phenomenal sum for the times.[19] He first worked in the county in 1765 when he made several journeys to Tong Castle, bought in 1764 by George Durant, who had made his fortune in the West Indies and as Paymaster to the forces in the Cuban expedition of 1762 - the latter celebrated by renaming a local hamlet 'Tong Havannah'.[20] Exactly how much of what was done at Tong can be attributed to Brown is uncertain, but by Durant's death in 1780 there had been great changes. The house itself was rebuilt in an extravagant mixture of Gothick and Moorish styles, and its old formal landscape of avenues and wilderness replaced by a far more open, pastoral one, in which water played a much greater part in the form of two great new sheets of water, Lodge Lake and Norton Mere. The park was entered past the picturesque Convent Lodge, which most commentators seem confident in ascribing to Brown, its staggered rear wall and gothick details intended to give the effect of a ruined monastery. The Hon. John Byng, however, a man of independent mind and blunt expression who rode through Shropshire in 1792, was unimpressed when he visited, either with house or garden. Tong Castle was 'pompous' and 'overgrown', lacking a library and with its every part covered with pictures procured from Christie's and other auctions: 'of dying saints, naked Venuses and drunken baccanals', an 'offensive show, disgusting to every English eye that has not been hardened to Italy.' Although Byng was prepared to commend the pleasure ground behind the house as 'pretty' and the serpentine lake as 'beautiful' he felt the latter capable of further improvement. 'Neither its banks or the park are half planted, but this is the case everywhere - views and wind form the present taste.'[21] Such an opinion is a salutory reminder that far from all in the later 18th century found the so-called natural style commendable, and also that the Brownian landscapes we see today, two hundred years on, are very different from those which contemporaries saw.

Fig. 38:
Tong Castle,
seen across its serpentine lake.
The landscape around it, in which
'Capability' Brown had a hand,
rivalled Hawkstone.

Brown next came to Shropshire in 1772 when he visited Lord Clive at Oakly Park, near Ludlow, but Clive's death in 1774 apparently put paid to any scheme which may have been in preparation.[22] As well as formal commissions there were probably numerous instances where he gave informal advice about improvements to friends and would-be clients. Such was probably the case when Brown came to Shropshire in the early 1770s to visit his friend Professor John Mainwaring, a Cambridge theologian (and later biographer of Handel) who from 1749 had held the rectory of Church Stretton. Although no plan survives it seems highly likely that the improvements which Mainwaring began about 1775 to the glebe were influenced by Brown, especially the planting up with trees of the pair of hills behind the parsonage, the laying out of walks, the modification of the brook down Townbrook Hollow and the formation of a dark, yew-ringed pool at its bottom. Those works were sufficiently ambitious for a mutual friend, Dr. Powell, Master of St. John's, to bequeath £200 for further improvements. Further works were done by Mainwaring's successors T.B. Coleman (rector 1807-18) and R.N. Pemberton (1818-48, the rebuilder of Millichope Park) who added various buildings and seats to the walks, and although few traces of those structures survive, Rectory Wood, which is owned by the county council, remains an attractive landscape to walk in.[23]

Buildings such as seats and summerhouses generally had a dual function, being pleasing additions to a landscape as well as providing shade or shelter for the visitor and a place where refreshment could be supplied. They also afforded a measure of privacy, always a valuable commodity in any household well provided with servants. Events at Petton, however, showed that there was little refuge from prying eyes when, in the course of the acrimonious divorce of Edward and Hannah Corbet, James Howell, sometime groom to Edward Corbet, deposed how on numerous occasions in the mid 1770s he had seen Edward Corbet and Anne Roberts the under-dairymaid go into the summerhouse in Corbet's garden. 'And he always observed that she went into the summerhouse one way and the said Edward went therein another way. The said deponent further says that he well remembers one evening in May in or about 1775 when he was in a fir tree standing close to the said summerhouse and concealed himself in the tree and then observed Edward and Anne go into the summerhouse. He looked through the window of the summerhouse the sash of which was up and then plainly observed the said Edward put his arms towards the clothes of the said Anne and then laid her down on the floor of the said summerhouse and then laid himself down. But they were then so low he could not see them and in about four or five minutes they both arose again and the said Edward then went out of the said summerhouse leaving her therein.'[24] Regrettably, both building and fir tree have long since disappeared.

By far the most important designer who worked in Shropshire in the later 18th century, and probably the most highly regarded, was William Emes (1730-1803). Emes's first commissions were in Staffordshire in the 1750s and were very much in the style of Brown. A serpentine lake was often the centrepiece of his designs - lakes and cascades were his specialities[25] - with clumps of trees and linear plantations being used both to add interest to the park and to shield unwanted intrusions such as the kitchen gardens and the world beyond the pale. Emes's first involvement in the county was at Aston Hall, near Oswestry, where in 1767 he produced a scheme for the Revd. William Lloyd, the principal features of which included a serpentine lake and, in the corner of the park, 'Mount Sinai', a tree covered hill. In the event nothing was done until 1780, the final scheme substituting a T-plan lake in place of Emes's initial suggestion.[26]

By the time he finally began work at Aston Emes was probably well known in the county through his employment by Clive's son at two estates purchased by his father: Oakly, where (perhaps as a cheaper alternative) he took over from Brown, and Walcot, near Lydbury North. He was at work at both by 1774, 'directing, planning and laying out'. Later accounts mention the planting of trees,

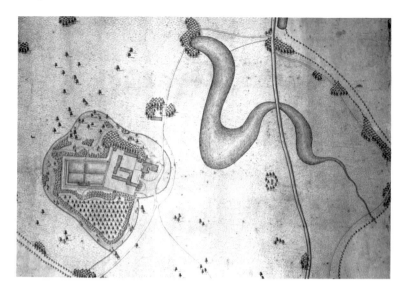

Fig. 39:
William Emes's 1767 scheme
for Aston Hall, near Oswestry.
A serpentine lake and clumps
of trees are proposed for the park,
but around the house are
paths and shrubberies.

the delivery of sheep from Leicester to Oakly, and the purchase of flowering shrubs from Brunton and Co., nurserymen of Birmingham. Unfortunately those accounts are far from complete and it is difficult to get a full picture of Emes's involvement at either place, although at least at Oakly he was still superintending operations as late as 1781.[27] It may be, for instance, that he was responsible for altering the existing pools at Walcot into the great lake which is such a feature of the park (Plate 27), for although tradition ascribes its excavation to Napoleonic prisoners of war, already in 1799 the visiting Richard Colt Hoare made note of a 'piece of water' before the house.[28]

In a number of other cases proposals by Emes went wholly, or largely unimplemented. That was probably the case with his next commission in Shropshire, a scheme of 1776 to improve the grounds of Lythwood Hall, near Shrewsbury, for the new owner Joshua Blakeway, a Shrewsbury draper who had won £20,000 on the National Lottery in 1794.[29] The same was apparently true of a plan produced in the following year for Dudmaston for William Whitmore, who two years previously had inherited the estate from the Wolryches. Here it seems the improvement and adornment of the Dingle to the south of the house with cascades, abutments, seats, niches and paths, may have owed more to Whitmore's wife Frances and their gardener 'Planter' Wood, the latter said to have 'imbibed his notions of taste at Shenstone's Leasowes'.[30] A scheme of 1783 to re-order the grounds of Cheswardine Hall (then called The Hill) for Henry Jervis apparently went no further,[31] and likewise proposals for Shavington. With another scheme, of 1784 for the grounds

Fig. 40:
Dudmaston Hall, where Emes's scheme
of 1777 was largely carried out by
Frances Whitmore and her gardener.

of Whitchurch Rectory,[33] further research will be needed before its influence can be assessed. Later, in 1786, a design by Emes was carried through at Hawkstone where in order to rectify Dr. Johnson's criticism that the place lacked water, Emes created the 3 km. long River Hawk, a canal-like lake below the house, planted up with trees on its lower side to give the impression that it lay in a valley bottom. Emes may also have been responsible for Hawkstone's other main sheet of water, Menagerie Pool, overlooked from the Elysian Hill.

Another estate visited by Emes,[35] although there is no record of any subsequent commission, was Halston, where in the 1770s Robert Mylne did work on the house for John Mytton, grandfather of the infamous 'Mad Jack'. That was part of a programme of improvements touching all aspects of the estate, economic and aesthetic, which Mytton was undertaking. Around the Hall the old, formal, layout was softened, clumps and plantations introduced - Black spruce, Scots pine, beech, wych elm, horse chestnuts and sycamores, for instance, all being planted in October 1780[36] - and a long, sinuous lake created from a by-passed length of the River Perry. This last undertaking well demonstrates just how great, both in scale and expense, such works could be. Probably designed by Thomas Slater,[37] a local surveyor, the lake was dug in two separate campaigns, with excavation of the west half beginning in June 1773 and continuing until 1775, while the east end, within which a 'great island' was formed, was dug between April 1777 and July 1778. In all Mytton reckoned 28,029 square yards (perhaps 40,000 tons) of earth had been excavated, and that the lake had cost some £530.[38] Once it was completed Mylne designed a 'wooden bridge on ropes', perhaps a mock suspension bridge, to go across it.[39]

Emes's most successful work in the county was probably at Badger where in the 1780s, in association with John Webb, he laid out the Dingle for Isaac Hawkins Browne.[40] Here, in a deep, thickly-wooded 2 km long natural ravine through the local red sandstone, he created a notable landscape planted, like the gardens of Badger Hall, with imported 'American' plants. Along the bottom of the Dingle three long pools were made separated by cascades, above which walks were contrived with caves, seats, and boathouses. At either end of the Dingle, served by drives from the house, was a Classical building: at one extremity the Rotunda, and at the other the Bird House (Plates 28-29). Both may have been designed by James Wyatt, who remodelled the hall between 1779 and 1783. The Rotunda, a circular stone temple, is a very typical form of garden building, and in Shropshire also appears at Millichope and Decker Hill. The Bird House is quite the reverse, and is a building of considerable ingenuity and distinction. It has a reception room or salon with apses to the front and rear, the former with folding glazed doors giving access to a semi-circular apron overlooking the landscape. In this room, whose hollow walls were heated greenhouse-style from fireplaces in the basement service room, exotic plants and caged songbirds would have been kept, just as described by the Classical writers so well known by Hawkins Browne.

Hardy North American species such as those planted by Emes at Badger became fashionable and comparatively easy to obtain from commercial nurseries in the later 18th century.[41] The style of garden created with the imports (although much propagation was, in fact, done from seed) varied widely: in some rhododendrons, magnolias, and camelias were used in formal beds, whereas in others liquidambers, swamp cypress or tulip trees were planted informally within a specific area. As many of the species were ericaceous - acid loving - peat, or 'bog earth' as it was sometimes called, had to be imported. As well as at Badger there were American gardens at Pitchford Hall, present by 1812,[42] at Acton Scott , created about 1815,[43] while at Dudmaston one was laid out in the earlier 20th century by Geoffrey Wolryche-Whitmore.[44] As is obvious to any garden visitor, rhododendrons are now widespread in almost every country house pleasure ground, testament to their continued popularity throughout the 19th century as well as, admittedly, to their resilience against all but the most drastic control measures. The ever widening range of specimen trees also encouraged the creation of arboretums, collections of different kinds of trees, sometimes with walks laid out around them. Probably the most celebrated in Shropshire is that at Walcot, which provides a backdrop to the Hall and extends in all to about 25 acres. It was developed in the early 19th century by Clive of India's son Edward, and includes among its firs, spruces and pines one of the Douglas firs grown from the first seeds supplied by the celebrated Scottish plant collector David Douglas in 1827 on his return from an expedition to Vancouver and Oregon. Another 19th-century arboretum is that at Hardwick, probably laid out in the later 1840s by Sir John Kynaston. Here again coniferous species predominated; indeed, in 1918 it was referred to as a 'pinetum', a specialist term for a collection of conifers.[45]

Emes's associate at Badger, John Webb (1754-1828), worked with him on various projects between 1782 and 1793, and is sometimes described as his pupil. He later established a large practice of his own, working mainly in the midlands and northern England. In Shropshire his commissions included Pradoe, bought in 1803 by the Hon. Thomas Kenyon and subject to various improvements by him in the following years including the creation of a lake and a pond and tree planting.[46]

Although best known, Emes was not the only local landscape gardener. Burlton Grove, near Wem, was the home of John Davenport, who also worked as an architect. He was employed in many parts of the country and in 1790, when he claimed to have been in business for 22 years, was specializing in 'hothouses, green houses etc.' One Shropshire commission was at Mawley Hall, where in the 1780s he produced drawings for a classical greenhouse, hothouse, orangery, lodge and gateway for Sir Walter Blount.[47] He also did work at Pitchford Hall in the 1780s although it is unknown whether he also contributed to the improvements to the grounds which were in progress at about that time.[48] Another man who presumably worked in the county, although probably more as contractor than designer, was Morris Sayce of Bishop's Castle. In 1809 he was in a partnership with James Stephens of Presteigne which advertized various surveying services among which was that pleasure grounds could be 'laid out upon the most approved modern plans'.[49] Finally, it was between 1769 and 1772 that the landscaping of the park at Attingham began, under the direction of Thomas Leggett, a well known Irish landscape designer whose manner was said to be 'pompous and dictatorial.'[50] Large sums were expended both on planting, of Scots pine, oak, elm, beech, flowering trees, shrubs and fruit trees, and on grading the slope down to the River Tern which was dredged and deepened.[51]

Fig. 41:
Morris Sayce's trade card.

By 1790, however, and within two years of deciding to take up the profession, England had a new leading practitioner of landscape design, Humphry Repton.[52] Born in 1752, Repton had had an early and unsuccessful business career before buying a small Norfolk estate and beginning to read widely on landscape gardening and botany. By 1788, however, his financial position was acute, and during a sleepless night he decided to take up the trade of landscape gardening which had lacked a recognized leader since the death of Brown in 1783. Within two years he was established and successful, not least because of the attractive way in which he presented his proposals to clients, usually as manuscript books incorporating views of the grounds with flaps to show how they would look after improvement. These books were usually bound in red leather, and by the time of his death in 1818 Repton had produced some 400 of them.

One of the very early commissions was at Ferney Hall near Ludlow, for which Repton produced a Red Book in 1791 for Samuel Peckham Phipps, who had bought the estate two years before.[53] Repton's ideas, such as sweeping away the existing terraces, creating a park between the house and Ducksmore Common, and throwing a bridge across a cavernous quarry above the house, met with criticism from his neighbour, the landscape theorist Richard Payne Knight of Downton Castle, and seem not to have been implemented. The two then agreed to produce a modified scheme and Repton visited again in 1790. The owner's enthusiasm, however, along with his health, were apparently failing, and although Phipps paid the cost of Repton's post chaise to Ferney his account remained unsettled and his involvement came to an end.

Other schemes in Shropshire seem to have had equally unsatisfactory conclusions, and there are doubts about whether any of Repton's ideas for either Shavington (for which a Red Book was produced in 1793) or Longner (1804) were acted upon.[54] At Attingham, for which he produced a Red Book for Lord Berwick in 1798, his proposals do seem to have been at least partly implemented. Here the main view from and of the house was improved by the broadening of the River Tern and by the introduction of trees in clumps and larger plantations, while to its side the park was extended to give greater privacy and gaps were opened in Leggett's shelter belts to give views out to the landscape beyond. That required that the hamlet of Berwick Maviston, with the exception of one house left as the home farm, be removed.[55] The full story has yet to be unravelled, but it seems unlikely that this was a sudden and forceable desertion like that described in Oliver Goldsmith's celebrated poem *The Deserted Village*. Instead it seems that as a lease came to an end it was not renewed, at which time the farmhouse would be demolished and its fields added to the park. Other proposals by Repton, however, for instance to make Tern bridge more monumental and to add a spire to the tower of Wroxeter church two miles away as an eye-catcher, went no further.[56]

Also involved in the works at Attingham was the architect John Nash, with whom Repton collaborated for a number of years after 1795. About 1800 he was brought in to improve the surrounds of the main entrance to the park at Atcham, which he did by adding gothick touches to several of the cottages there on the south side of the road and possibly knocking down a group on the north. Although less comprehensive than what he was to do with his model village of Blaise Hamlet, near Bristol, the Atcham scheme predates it by ten years.[57] In fact hereabouts there is a remarkable cluster of work by Nash: his triumphal arch of about 1807 at Atcham Lodge, through which Attingham's park was entered; a west, castellated, lodge to the same park, once more in the gothick style; and opposite the last a lodge of about 1805 to Longner Hall, an early experiment in the Tudor-Elizabethan style (Plate 30). Probably best known of the lodges here, however, is the angular stone Tern Lodge (Plate 31) on the north side of Watling Street opposite the turn to Wroxeter, which was intended to be one of a pair on opposite sides of the road which Repton hoped would 'induce the stranger to conceive that he passes thro' the park and not on the outside of it.'[58]

Fig. 42:
Nash's vision of Atcham
(seen here from the end of the bridge
across the Severn, looking east)
as a picturesque hamlet.
The gothicized cottage
second from left remains
instantly recognizable today.

In fact it was at about this time that the relationship between Repton and Nash was breaking down as the latter consistently failed to honour the spirit of their agreement. That notwithstanding, a business relationship between the two families continued until 1817 through Nash's employment of Repton's sons John Adey and George as collaborators and assistants, and while the precise date is uncertain it was probably John who designed Tern Lodge.[59] Although imperfectly documented it seems quite likely that one of the Reptons also had a hand in laying out the grounds of Hopton Court, just outside Hopton Wafers, where Thomas Botfield apparently brought in Nash to remodel the house in the Italian style.[60] In 1855 Botfield's grandson wrote a description of the house, noting that 'The grounds, formed under the direction of Mr. Repton, are adapted to the course of the dingle, and by the means of walks all its parts are easily accessible.'[61] That scheme had apparently been preferred to one proposed by the precocious Scottish garden writer John Loudon which he featured in his *Treatise on Improving Country Residences*, published in 1806 when he was only 23 years old.[62]

One feature of the improvements at Hopton was the closure of roads which ran close to the house in order to increase its privacy. Such clearances, not only of long established roads tracks and paths but also of houses and indeed all traces of mundane human activity from the idealized world of the park, were quite common in the 18th and earlier 19th centuries, and a number of other examples can be given from Shropshire. At Longnor, for instance, Archdeacon Plymley created a new 73-acre landscape park very soon after he came in to the property in 1774, sweeping away the old formal gardens and having the Shrewsbury - Hereford road diverted away from the Hall by order of the Quarter Sessions (Plate 32).[63] A similar scheme, with roads diverted, hedges grubbed and at least one house demolished, was undertaken at Hawkstone about 1790.[64] More extreme was what happened at Willey where in the years after 1811 a 270-acre landscape park (Plate 33) was laid out around the socially ambitious Cecil Weld Forester's new Hall.[65] Here roads were closed and diverted, the thriving hamlet of Hangstree Gate deserted, and the nearby 17th-century Slaney almshouses and school demolished and replaced by new buildings in Barrow village out of sight of the Hall. John Cox, Forester's tenant at Willey farm, complained of the expense that imparkment had caused him as he was forced to take down fences, fill in ditches, and put down arable to grass. All that was retained were some of the hedgerow trees, which would have provided welcome points of maturity and interest in what was otherwise a raw and young landscape. Much the same was done at about the same time at Attingham, where the village of Berwick Maviston was removed, as well as about 15 years later at Acton Reynald, where again a rebuilding programme at the Hall was accompanied by removal of the old crossroads village which adjoined it, imparkment, and road realignment.[66]

The growing seclusion of the gentry was further enhanced, and indeed announced, by the proliferation of lodges at the end of drives. Most were small, and as trumpets of their owner's status many had external architectural elaboration to rival the great house. The employment of leading architects was common, whether a lodge was part of a general estate building programme or a commission in its own right. Most later 18th- and early 19th-century examples are small, single-storey, and broadly in the Classical idiom. Typical are those built about 1800 at Haughton Hall, Shifnal, about 1810 at William Botfield's new house at Decker Hill, also just outside Shifnal,[67] or slightly later at Millichope.[68] In fact so ubiquitous is the style that the few departures from it, such as the gothick west lodge of about 1760 at Downton Hall,[69] are noteworthy and refreshing whatever their individual shortcomings. Among the few grand entrances to Shropshire houses is Nash's entrance screen of about 1807 to Attingham Park, and Benjamin Gummow's Triumphal arch of 1815 which heralded the presence of Brogyntyn to all who passed on their way to Oswestry.[70]

A landscape park was attractive to a landowner in many ways. As well as demonstrating in a highly visible fashion the elite status of his family it also insulated them from visible reminders of many of the realities of life. It could also be (as long as lake digging was avoided) cheap to lay out - there were many books available to assist a gentlemen who wished to be his own designer - and maintained at virtually no cost, with the grassland being grazed either by the owners's own stock or even let for a profit. Few could deny, however, that many parks were bland to the point of dullness, a criticism voiced by contemporary writers. John Byng, for instance, was scathing about Attingham, finding the Hall a 'great tasteless seat, a thing like the Mansion House', and the surrounds 'in most deplorable taste: trees in clumps; water designed and not finished; and within a short distance of a great town.'[71] Even those who worked quite closely in the style of Brown himself seem to have accepted such criticisms, and Emes's designs, for instance, at least gave the client the opportunity to retain some beds or shrubs around the house. At Lythwood his plan included a roughly circular enclosure around the Hall labelled as 'small inclosure to be kept as Pleasure garden with green house etc. if required.'[72] At Aston Hall he actually provided designs for elaborate pleasure grounds with flower beds, shrubberies and twisting paths around the house to provide colour, interest, and amusement. Byng, however, could not see these from the road, and remained unimpressed by Aston: 'the grounds are staringly laid open - in the modern taste, with mean clumps of firs, and larches.'[73]

*Fig. 43:
Lythwood Hall,
for which Emes
produced a scheme of
improvements in 1776.*

Although Repton's work was more varied than Brown's, and later even had elements of formality using balustrades, steps, and trellised enclosures for flowers, it too attracted a number of critics. Chief among those were two north Herefordshire landowners, Richard Payne Knight of Downton Castle and Sir Uvedale Price of Foxley, who in the 1790s instead proposed new concepts of landscape appreciation and especially the importance of the picturesque. Heavily influenced by the work of fashionable continental artists such as Claude Lorraine, Gaspar Poussin, and Salvator Rosa - in Shropshire there were Rosa's paintings at Halston, Sundorne, and at Orleton where the Cluddes had four[74] - in place of pastoral shaven lawns and clumps of trees they advocated scenery that was more varied and rugged, and the celebration of the drama and wildness of nature with cliffs, cascades, and wooded hillsides. It is indicative of the depth and sophistication of the debate that a clear distinction was made between on the one hand 'picturesque' landscapes and on the other 'sublime' ones such as Hawkstone, the latter being ones which inspired awe and provoked thoughts of dread and eternity.

One Shropshire landscape perhaps directly infuenced by the proponents of the new ideas on the picturesque[75] was that at The Lodge, two miles south of Ludlow.[76] This was a small estate owned by Theophilus Salwey, a member of a well-established Ludlow family who was acquainted with Price and Knight, both of whom lived only a short ride away. Salwey's house was rebuilt in the 1780s on the lip of a dingle, above which rose the wooded hills of Haye Park wood and Bringewood Chase. By 1812 Salwey's planting of the dingle was becoming well known, with its striking variety of specimen trees among which, even to this day, the Blue fir stand out. Along the bottom of the valley there were pools, a cascade and rill, and a bath house set against the valley side. Paths ran through and above the dingle, at one end of which and overlooking it was a seat which also gave magnificent views across to the rugged profile of the Clee Hills. The whole is very reminiscent of the valley elysiums at Knight's estates of Croft and Downton and it is likely that, even if Knight gave no formal assistance in designing the Lodge dingle, Salwey had his work in mind.

The bath house at the Lodge was one of several, perhaps even many, constructed in Shropshire in the later 18th century. In 1707 a Dr. Oliver published *A Practical Dissertation on the Bath Waters*, which promoted weekly or monthly cold baths as condusive to a healthy and robust constitution. The theory apparently gained wide acceptance, and gentlemen soon began to build them in their park or garden, where, as Mark Girouard has argued, they could be made the object of an afternoon's outing.[77] The earliest example known in Shropshire is a so-called well at Blodwell Hall

Fig. 44:
The Lodge, at Overton near Ludlow.
The dingle below the house was planted
up in the years around 1800 in a way
which was heavily influenced by the ideas
of Richard Payne Knight.

approached by steps and served (if antiquarian report is to be believed) by hot and cold water pipes from the house, presumably dating from the time of the Bridgemans' improvement of Blodwell's grounds in the years around 1700 and certainly from before when, about 1720, the family gave up the house.[78] However, until the reign of George III a proclivity for the invigorating cold plunge apparently remained rare in the county, and most of the known examples - and in passing it may be noted how many of those are in the Oswestry area - probably date from twenty years either side of 1800. The baths themselves, usually taking advantage of a natural spring, are often little more than tanks, usually about three metres square and a metre deep, their water crystal clear and bitingly cold. At the Lodge the building which contains the bath is of stone, with a central entry, the bath to one side and a small changing room to the other. At Hawkstone a 'spacious' cold bath (already disused by 1832) with a solid stone table in the centre with stone seats around it was in a building later known as the summerhouse.[79] Other bath houses were of wood, as perhaps at Woodhouse,[80] Wood Hill,[81] and Park Issa,[82] all near Oswestry, while some may have lain open to the elements. There are, for instance, no signs of buildings over the surviving baths at Aston Hall, Pitchford, Tyn-y-Rhos,[83] or Ferney, although the last adjoins a summerhouse with a fireplace (Plate 34), no doubt a place 'for taking some self-congratulatory refreshment after the plunge.'[84] All these lie at some distance from the house, and often concealed by or in a wood or a declivity in the ground, no doubt to give greater privacy to the bathers.[85]

If there was one thing that garden designers agreed upon in the 18th century, whatever else they thought about the true nature of a beautiful landscape, it was that the kitchen garden should be well hidden. It is paradoxical that this increasing denial of the existence of the workaday garden occurred at just the time that their produce was becoming a key indicator of the owner's status. In the Middle Ages and beyond the kitchen garden, where fruits, salad greens and other vegetables of the best quality and freshness were produced, was usually but one of several garden compartments clustered around the house. In the later 17th century, as was seen in the last chapter, greenhouses and heated walls began to appear, and with this a tendency, as at Berwick, north of Shrewsbury, for the kitchen gardens to be moved close to the stables in order to reduce the distance that dung had to be carted. This separation of the working garden, favoured also by the more ambitious designers of formal layouts, became more pronounced as the new ideas of Brown and his contemporaries gained favour. Kitchen gardens, along with other utilitarian buildings such as stables, were further concealed by the use of belts of trees, as introduced by Emes at Aston and by Repton at Attingham. Nevertheless, pragmatic owners, and even more their cooks and gardeners, realized that while a distance of hundred yards or so between house and walled garden would do much for the former's setting, more would be impractical given that often weighty and bulky produce would daily have to be taken to the kitchen. At Halston this very mistake was made when the kitchen gardens were moved as part of landscape improvements there in the 1760s and 1770s. In fact, not only were they moved almost a half mile from the house they were also put next to a public road; with hindsight John Mytton, the owner, recognized fully the problems, not only of logistics but also of security.[86] Security in general seems to have been an increasing concern at this time, and as he passed Attingham John Byng mused how, were it his, he would build a wall around the park 'as high as walls could be built, to keep out insolence and roguery.'[87]

Mytton gave a good deal of thought to the practicalities of the kitchen garden, and about 1777, six years before his death, set down his thoughts for the benefit of his son, still then a minor.[88] A 'reasonable' supply of fruit and vegetables was certainly required, and 'makes everyone relish their meat, but too great abundance will surfeit and become a real waste.' He reckoned that for an acre of kitchen garden seeds, tools, wages, manure and carriage would amount to £25 a year: 'at this rate peas and salads are dear.' Nevertheless, such gardens were about more than economics, and the range and quality of their produce, when served to guests, did much to establish the status and largesse of the owner. At Halston, for instance, as well as the more everyday fruits and vegetables the gardens had melon, cucumber and mushroom beds, strawberries, gooseberries and currants.

One expenditure which Mytton apparently avoided was a hothouse. Again he had done his sums, concluding 'to build a hothouse as glass is now so dear a commodity [is improvident]; the value of ten guineas will probably purchase in London more Pine Apples (a fruit which carries well and keeps a good while) than a common hothouse, if not very judiciously managed, is likely to produce at an expense of £50 a year.' Glass's high price was due to the heavy duty payable on it, and glasshouses and conservatories of late 18th and early 19th century date are fairly unusual, while those that were built were generally sparing in their use of glass. There were, however, exceptions. Walcot's seems to have been a household which valued its fruit and in 1790, by when there was already a greenhouse and a hot house, a 'hot walk' was being planned, and Robert Gardner was sent to Kew 'to take the dimensions' of one in the royal gardens. During the next year the work continued at Walcot; a peach house was built in the garden and peach and nectarine trees bought for forcing.[89] At Apley Park a valuation of 1795[90] shows that in the kitchen gardens, new walled[91] and probably among the largest in the county (Plate 35), were a peach house and

Fig. 45:
The orangery at Hopton Court,
near Hopton Wafers. The curving glass and
iron structure is built against a heated wall,
the vents of which can be seen running between
the two ornamental chimneys.

Fig. 46:
The conservatory at Acton Scott.
Hazel Fryer suggests the drawing
may be in the style of
John Adey Repton.

a pair of hot houses, the older of the two with 32 top lights each 10 ft. 3 in. long by 3 ft. 6 in. wide and the same number of front lights each 2 ft. 10 in. tall. The presence of 64 vine poles hints at one of their main crops. Most telling was that in addition to the glass houses, and to 43 hand glasses, there were 125 'light boxes' - that is cold frames - 83 of them 9 ft. by 5 ft. and the rest 7 ft. by 4 ft. 6 in. Such profligate employment of glass in the garden at this time is remarkable.

Normally, as has been said, it was used more frugally. Nash's gothick conservatory at Longner, part of the rebuilt house of about 1805, is more stone than glass, while equally integral to the house are Lewis Wyatt's conservatory at Willey of about 1815, C.R. Cockerell's at Oakly Park of 1824 and Sir Jeffry Wyatville's orangery at Lilleshall of about 1830. At Walcot the use of glass was more lavish, and by 1822 a long, curving hot house had been built off the end of the ballroom, probably using mass produced components from Birmingham. Charles Hulbert, the Shrewsbury writer and publisher, thought it 'the most spacious and costly [hot house] I ever beheld.'[92] Exactly when this was built is uncertain, and it is not impossible that it was the 'hot walk' being planned in 1790. All those were additions to houses of the grandest sort. At what might be termed gentry houses notable freestanding orangeries were built at Hopton Court and at Deckerhill, the latter, sadly demolished many years ago, apparently manufactured by the same firm responsible for the well-known example at Barton Seagrave in Northamptonshire. Both the Hopton Court and Decker Hill examples are undocumented, although in both cases a date in or about the 1830s seems likely. At a more modest establishment, Acton Scott Hall, a heated conservatory was added to the side of the Hall in 1817, during a programme of modernization put in hand by Thomas Stackhouse and his young wife Frances.[93] Remarkably this survives much as when depicted in an early 19th-century watercolour, with raised beds, a stone-flagged floor, artificial rockery, and decorative wooden trellising. Originally, as the watercolour shows, the dominant component of the planting was flowering plants and climbers.

The number of gardeners needed to maintain even a modest kitchen garden of an acre or two was considerable. Moreover, their attendance on the garden, to water, to stoke boilers, and to open and shut hoppers and shutters, required that they be housed close to it and many gardens had a dormitory or 'bothy' for the under-gardeners constructed nearby or even as an integral part of the walled garden. At Attingham a single-storey brick bothy with fireplace and attic was built

Fig. 47: Halston, with its expensive lake to the right.

Plate 30: Longner Hall, John Nash's lodge of about 1805.

*Plate 31: Tern Lodge, Attingham Park, probably designed
by John Adey Repton.*

*Plate 32: The park at Longnor, near Dorrington, was created by
Archdeacon Plymley in the later 1770s.*

*Plate 33: Willey Park, painted by J. H. Smith in 1827,
not long after the house was completed
and the new park laid out.*

Plate 34: The cold bath (left) and summerhouse at Ferney Hall, Ludlow.

Plate 35:
Apley Park's huge
kitchen gardens,
probably of about 1795,
include a pair of small
buildings. They were
probably for the storage
of garden produce,
and perhaps seeds.

Plate 36: Ludlow's Castle Walks, laid out in 1772,
were painted very soon afterwards by William Morlowe.
Figures can be seen on the hillside path.

against the outer wall - a typical location - when the walled garden was rebuilt in the 1780s, while in 1914 at Park Hall, Oswestry, the 'bothy' was stone built, slate roofed and provided accomodation for seven men with a mess room, larder, sitting room and three large bedrooms.[94] Also built on to the walled garden, as at Pell Wall (1820s) and at Leaton Knolls (under constuction 1851),[95] and overlooking it like a medieval gatehouse, might be a more substantial house for the head or under-under gardener.

At Halston, clearly a well-ordered household, a book was kept in the 1750s which contained the duties of every servant, to be read aloud when any new employee joined the 'Halston family'. The gardener's duties were to see that the garden was properly planted and kept clear of weeds, leaving part fallow every year in order to save manure. He was to superintend the mowing of the shrubbery, walks and wood, to rear all sorts of deciduous and coniferous trees and shrubs, and to raise most kinds of seeds for the kitchen garden. He was also to be responsible for filling the icehouse with ice, and for the care of the fishing nets if no gamekeeper was employed. Finally, in the winter months and at other spare times he was to superintend the garden labourers in making baskets and beesoms for use in the gardens.[96]

The independence which gardeners enjoyed, as well as their enjoyment of traditional perks of the job, provided ample scope for misunderstandings between themselves and others. In the later 18th century the Whitmores' demands for exotic fruits from their greenhouses and hot beds at Apley and the failure of successive gardeners to supply them lead to a rapid turnover of staff. In May 1791 Thomas Barnfield, the agent there, notified Thomas Whitmore that the cucumber and melon crops had failed; red spiders were said to be to blame. Both the gardener and the agent knew the likely outcome, and Barnfield wrote to his master with the gardener's reaction advising Whitmore that 'if you determine to dismiss him, he thinks you will better suit yourself with another while you are in town.' If Barnfield was sympathetic in this particular instance it did not mean he was well disposed towards gardeners as a whole, and in 1780 he wrote to Whitmore concerning yet another new gardener, opining that he 'should not have the liberty of selling anything of your garden, which is the custom often practised to such a degree as to make the produce of a garden come sparingly into a kitchen; also such privileges make Gardeners cry out for more room.'[97]

Fig. 48: Whitehall, Shrewsbury, where Thomas Brocas became gardener in 1786.

If the gardener was like Thomas Brocas one's sympathies are entirely with the owners as, with his head full of methodism, Brocas daydreamed through life. In February 1786 he was in trouble with 'master' at Sansaw because he had failed to fill the icehouse and no ice was available for iced foods and drinks at the evening's party or 'rout', and three months later with 'Mrs.' who 'came through the garden and finding most of the green house plants dead by the frost spoke to me very sharply.' Later that year he left Sansaw after eight years and became gardener to Mr. Wingfield at Whitehall, in Shrewsbury. The post was not ideal, and in his diary he complained that whereas at Sansaw he had been accustomed to eat with the head servants and was given tea for breakfast, here he was put down with the under-servants. While his pay was less than the £20 a year he had hoped he was to enjoy the perk of selling surplus garden stuffs which would take his salary up to £20 or even 20 guineas. To begin with things seem to have gone quite well, and in August 1787 on his return to Whitehall after a visit elsewhere Mr. Wingfield commended Brocas on how well everything looked, praising his melons as the best he ever tasted. Two years later, however, exasperated by his preaching activities, the Wingfields sacked Brocas and he gave up gardening.[98]

Brocas's initial training was in a nursery garden, and these proliferated both in number and in scope in the late 18th century. Tree nurseries were already established in most parts of the country by the mid 18th century and it has even been argued that by 1748 there would have been one in every large town and village in the country.[99] In Shropshire the example has already been given of Thomas Wright of Bicton, who in 1719 supplied the trees for the Quarry in Shrewsbury. Other tree nurserymen included John Bell of Burcott who was active in the 1730s (below), John Heels of The Riddings, near Ludlow, whose stock in 1786 included fruit trees, Weymouth pines and beeches,[100] John Lokiers of Stanton Lacy, supplier of cider apple trees in 1790,[101] and Mr. Cornwall of Diddlebury, who in 1791 supplied 46 fir trees to the vicar of Eaton-under-Heywood.[102] By 1800, as new plants were introduced from abroad and the public's interest in horticulture and botany increased, the range of species on offer expanded greatly and new men entered the trade. One such was Richard Colley (or Collis) of Betton, whose catalogue offered, among much else, 24 forest trees and 97 flowering shrubs.[103] Among the best customers would have been the inhabitants of the villas and suburbs which were appearing around towns in the early 19th century, and it is interesting that it was specifically to 'ladies' that the Shrewsbury seedsmen C. Bigg and Son of Pride Hill addressed their advertisement of 1829[104] offering 'Dutch Flower Roots' including hyacinths, as well as trees, evergreen and deciduous shrubs, greenhouse and American plants, double dahlias, pinks and carnations.

By the time Brocas arrived in Shrewsbury the lime avenues in the Quarry were mature and it had become well known as a place for the quality to meet.[105] Improvements, moreover, were still being made by the Corporation; large amounts of soil were brought in for landscaping purposes, and fashionable blue-painted wooden gothick seats installed. Not infrequently, however, these had to be recovered from the Severn where they had been pitched by drunken revellers, and repaired. Another recurring problem was damage to the trees, again it seems usually on Saturday nights, although the greatest act of arboreal vandalism was perpetrated in 1793 by Mr. Rock, the mayor, who after purchasing General Severn's house at the bottom of Quarry Place cut down sixteen limes in the middle walk in order to open a view from his house to Frankwell. 'There they lay like dead men', a contemporary noted, 'and I ready to weep over them.' Later, in 1790, the whole of the top walk was cut down and the town walls demolished in order to make way for the rebuilding of St. Chad's church. More generally offensive to the well-to-do seems to have been the fact that the Quarry continued to be used by the townsmen as it had been for hundreds of years, as grazing for cows and horses and as a drying ground both for newly manufactured cloth and for bloomers and sheets laundered by Shrewsbury's washerwomen. In 1829 a correspondent to the *Shrewsbury*

Chronicle complained the Quarry was the '*rendezvous* of washerwomen, and the daily <u>exhibition</u> of garments, from the modest chemise to the inexpressible breeches ... vast sheets and counterpains seem as many blots on a beautiful picture.' In 1834 a committee was established, perhaps more in hope than expectation, to 'devize the best means of preventing the nuisance occasioned by persons hanging linen on the Quarry trees to dry, and of pointing out a proper place for that purpose.'

By the early 19th century public walks and gardens had begun to appear elsewhere in Shropshire, many the gifts of private benefactors. In Bridgnorth, perhaps echoing what had been done twenty years earlier in Shrewsbury, John Bell, a nurseryman of Burcott (in Wrockwardine), was engaged in 1739 to plant a walk of two lines of elm, lime and chestnut trees, each at least twelve feet high, at Bernard's Hill in the Low Town, from which spectacular views were to be had of the cliff on which High Town stood and the long-established walks around it.[106] In Ludlow the Earl of Powis bought the castle in 1771 to save it from ruin, and in the following year his wife paid for the laying out of the Castle Walks (Plate 36). Those took well-to-do Ludlovians through ornamental grounds and then along paths cut into the precipitous slopes behind the castle, whose ruins reared high above them while below the waters of the Teme roared over rapids.[107] In 1799 George Lipscomb said the walks were 'kept with great neatness', and that they 'afford an interesting and agreeable promenade.'[108] Churchyards, too, saw what might be termed amenity planting. At Whitchurch St. Alkmund's, the fine new church of 1712-13, had a row of specimen trees planted along the south side of its churchyard before the mid century,[109] while by 1793 at Oswestry there were rows of lime trees in the churchyard beneath whose shade the Hon. John Byng walked and listened to the bees humming.[110] Churchwardens' accounts indicate similar improvements to churchyards in Shrewsbury.

Perhaps the most unusual walks were those created on Lincoln Hill, between Coalbrookdale and Ironbridge, by Richard Reynolds the eminent Quaker ironmaster.[111] The walks were laid out after he purchased the manor of Madeley in 1780-81,[112] and in 1852 his granddaughter recalled

> '*having made considerable purchases of land ... he had great enjoyment in planting and improving these estates, and laying out walks through the woods. Those upon Lincoln Hill, which were of some extent, were made expressly for the workmen, and seats were put up at different points, where they commanded beautiful views; they were called "The Workmen's walks", and were a source of much innocent enjoyment, especially on a Sunday, when the men, accompanied by their wives and children, were induced to spend the afternoon or evening there, instead of at the public house.'*

The seats included a Doric temple overlooking Upper Forge Pool[113] and a rotunda, on the summit of Lincoln Hill, which formed the main focus of the walks. This was clearly a construction of some ingenuity, perhaps manufactured in the Coalbrookdale works themselves, supported on seven iron pillars and with a moveable seat 'being the segment of a circle, fastened in the centre by a pin, and moves upon three wheels, running upon a circular wooden ring and easily moved in any direction forming a screen to the wind.' The planting included firs, larches and a variety of shrubs and evergreens, and to one early 19th-century visitor an equal of the 'romantic and picturesque' walks and the views down the Dale to the Ironbridge Gorge was scarcely to be found.[114] In the event the walks probably did not long survive Reynolds's departure from Shropshire in 1804, and indeed the demolition of the rotunda before the year was ended suggests they were done away with as soon as he left.[115] Was it that for those in the Dale with land and property workmen's walks represented a threat to the natural order, even perhaps of sedition?

Fig. 49:
Richard Reynolds, Quaker ironmaster
and philanthropist.

Fig. 50:
The Doric temple, in Coalbrookdale Workmen's Walks,
in the late 19th century. The brick side wall hints at
the jerry-built nature of most garden buildings.

A Return to Formality: 1820-80

Good taste, in no small manner, is knowing when to stop. At Tong the Durants did not, and treated the landscape as a cabinet of curiosities which required filling. George Durant, who had brought in Capability Brown to redesign the house and park, died in 1780 and was succeeded by his son, also George.[1] He was only four, but as soon as he came of age he carried on what his father had begun, adorning not only his own grounds but also the farms of his tenants with structures united only by their eccentricity. A new and elaborate entrance was built in 1821 at Convent Lodge, where Brown's picturesque lodge was overwhelmed by gate piers and flanking walls which the architectural historian Christopher Hussey described as carrying 'an almost Hindu weight of luxuriant ornament.' Fragments still remain, with carved butterflies and other devices, but sadly demolished is the stone gazebo, modelled on the pulpit at Shrewsbury Abbey, in which Durant is said to have sat and conversed with passers by. As visitors came up the drive and alongside a wooded dingle they passed pedestals topped with balls and urns, and under arches contrived from whale bones and surmounted with 'Aeolian harps' designed to make etherial sounds as the wind blew through them. Nearer the house was a wooden, windowless hut, whose interior was painted black and adorned with luminous demons and in which the Durants' naughty children

Fig. 51:
The replica of the pulpit at Shrewsbury Abbey
built at the entrance to Tong Castle
in the early 19th century.

73

would be locked. They might also see a weeping willow tree on the south lawn. This was manufactured of cast iron and contained secret pipes which spurted water from the leaves drenching any visitor unfortunate enough to sit on the seat at its base. Such joke fountains were essentially a 17th-century fashion, but they clearly saw a limited revival in the early 19th century and Paxton, for instance, installed an elaborate copper and brass version at Chatsworth about 1830.[2] Many of the features at Tong - as indeed at Hawkstone which may have provided the model - were embellished with inscriptions of an improving and humorous nature, a practice also carried on elsewhere on the Tong estate. Pyramids seem to have been a particular favourite: a brick one was built to house the hens at Vauxhall Farm (Plate 37), while a cottager on an island in Norton Mere was provided with a sandstone one four metres high as a privy, over the door of which was inscribed *parva sed apta*, 'small but necessary'.

Had Tong Castle and its landscape survived they would have been celebrated, even if undeniably vulgar. Sadly, however, time, neglect, and deliberate demolition have all played their part in the destruction of Tong. That began on the night in 1844 when George Durant (II) died. His sons marched to Knoll Hill, east of Norton Mere, and blew up an octagonal, three-storey cottage thereon, erected by their father about 1820 to celebrate a reduction in the amount of alimony he was required to pay to his divorced wife. Little now remains at Tong, and in the 1970s the M54 motorway was driven across the site of the castle, whose remains had been blown up in 1954. Sadly such a fate, even if not in quite such a sudden and violent fashion, has met all too many of the county's 19th-century parks and gardens.

It must, in fact, be said at the outset that to speak of 19th-century fashions in landscape design and gardening is misleadingly simple, and that the century saw a wide variety of styles in vogue at various times, and indeed simultaneously. There is a good deal of argument, for instance, about the so-called gardenesque, and to what extent this can be called a distinct fashion. In practice the gardenesque style was a mixing together of the formal and the informal, employing straight lines around the house and other 'hard' landscape features but using alongside them flower beds, trees and shrubs and a generous provision of garden buildings and seats in a variety of styles. If one ignores the contemporary polemical writers on gardening and looks at the evidence of individual gardens themselves, especially ordinary ones in the provinces, this is what most gardens had long comprised anyway. However, it certainly is true that, at least in the pleasure grounds immediately around houses, the earlier 19th century saw a revival in formality, increasingly derived from ideas about the historic past. Bedding out schemes filled many of those formal gardens with masses of garishly coloured and regimentally organized flowers, especially from the 1840s when the price of glass fell and glasshouses proliferated as never before or since. At the same time there was an increasing interest in botanical gardening and in horticulture as a science, and many new trees, shrubs and flowers made their appearance in the garden. Beyond the pleasure ground, in the private park, little changed, although it probably is true to say that the number of entrance lodges, for which the gothic style was increasingly seen as the most appropriate, continued to grow as landowners' concerns with privacy and with the protection of game grew to new heights. In towns public parks became increasingly common, many of them provided by philanthropic corporations and individuals.

Although the term 'gardenesque' was not coined, by J.C. Loudon, until 1832,[3] the new pleasure grounds laid out around Acton Scott Hall in the 15 years after T.P. Stackhouse arrived there as resident lord in 1807 were very much in that style. In front of the Hall, to which a dining room and conservatory were added, flower beds were dug into the 17th-century bowling green lawn, coniferous and other specimen trees were planted around its edge with a shrubbery beyond,

Fig. 52:
The garden front of Acton Scott
Hall, drawn soon after the
property's improvement
by the Stackhouses.

and new walks and drives laid out to the church and public roads. Large numbers of cast iron urns for flowers were purchased from a foundry, an American garden created in 'bog earth', while before 1830 an old stone quarry in the shrubbery west of the main drive had been turned into a Rock, or Quarry, garden. Hedges were grubbed up to open up views from the Hall and to create a small park, and over 35,000 larch, Scots pine and Canadian poplar were obtained from nurseries in London and Scotland for planting around the grounds and on the estate in general.

Stackhouse and his wife Frances were probably their own designers, from 1810 working with Thomas Cole, their newly hired gardener. Both came from families with strong traditions of enquiry into the natural sciences, and indeed may have first become acquainted through their fathers' shared interests.[4] Frances was the more local, and was the elder, and favourite, daughter of Thomas Andrew Knight of Downton Castle (Herefordshire) and the niece of his brother Richard Payne Knight, proponent of the picturesque. T.A. Knight was one of the most celebrated researchers of the age into pomology, vegetable physiology and plant breeding. He was elected a Fellow of the Royal Society in 1805 and from 1811 until his death in 1838 was President of the Horticultural Society of London. At Downton and in London Frances met many of the leading scientific figures of the age, such as the 'gouty' old baronet Sir Joseph Banks, and Sir Humphrey Davy, who in 1811 caused some amusement by arriving at Downton accompanied by a rich widow, Mrs. Preece (whom he later married) 'a blue stocking widow ... showy in person, handsomly dressed and highly rouged.' His fame, and her fortune, Frances surmised, were the bedrocks of their relationship. T.A. Knight's best known work *Pomona herefordiensis* was published in 1811; Frances supplied the drawings on which three of its plates were based, and in her memoirs remembered how she would often sit happily with her father 'by the fire in his study, while I helped him by copying the papers sent to the Royal, or Horticultural Society.'[5] Thomas Pendarves Stackhouse, the Cornishman whom she married the following year when just 18 years old, also had a father with scientific interests. Those were focussed on seaweed, and between 1795 and 1801 John Stackhouse published the three parts of his *Nereis britannica*, important not only as the first major study of the common seaweeds of the British Isles but also in the history of botany in general for its break from Linnaean nomenclature. Little wonder that the young couple set to with a will at Acton Scott as soon as they were married, or that during his first summer of married life Thomas also joined the Horticultural Society and bought and had bound a back run of their *Transactions*.[6]

Something of a link between what had gone before, and the fashions which were to dominate the mid 19th century, is provided by alterations to the grounds at Hawkstone. The estate had been inherited in 1824 by Sir Rowland Hill, the 2nd Viscount, who signalled his intention to modernize by calling in the architect Lewis Wyatt to remodel the Hall. Eight years later his attention turned to its pleasure grounds, and he invited William Sawrey Gilpin to devize proposals for a new layout.[7] Gilpin's general approach to landscape design was a modified version of picturesque principles as espoused by his uncle and teacher William Gilpin, and was undoubtedly dated by 1832, the year he published *Practical Hints upon Landscape Gardening*. Even W.S. Gilpin, however, was prepared to concede one point, that the 18th-century removal of terraces from around houses was aesthetically destructive; it was now agreed that a house required architectural separation from its park, and Gilpin began to include balustrades, terraces and steps in his designs.[8] Quite how much he actually did in Shropshire, however, is far from clear. The visit to Hawkstone was aborted because of gout, Gilpin instead returning home and reporting that 'my medical man gives me no hope of moving ... between this and the 10th [of September].'[9] Although he may later have returned to advize on either the new pleasure grounds which lay north and east of the Hall, or on the park extensions, any such assistance for the moment remains undocumented. Four years later the Duchess of Sutherland was hoping that she could get Gilpin over for the day to Lilleshall Hall, which in the later 1820s had been remodelled and much enlarged by Sir Jeffry Wyatville who had also designed a terrace with balustrade to the south and west of it and an orangery. 'I think he [Gilpin] will be of great use to us,' she wrote, 'in planting some of the banks near the house, on our approaches, & in a new drive that we are making. I feel sure that we shall do this better and more rapidly for having him.' Her hopes though remained unrealized, certainly for a year or more, and while it may be that in due course Gilpin did assist with the work at Lilleshall, at least in 1837 the duchess was feeling disillusioned and let down.[10]

Fig. 53:
The uppermost terrace at Oteley,
photographed about 1860.

Plate 37: Vauxhall Farm, Tong: the pyramidal hen house.

Plate 38: Hawkstone in 1824,
the year it was inherited by Sir Rowland Hill.

*Plate 39: The gardeners at Oteley,
photographed about 1880. The bowler-hatted figure is
presumably Salusbury Kynaston Mainwaring, the owner.*

*Plate 40: Oteley today, arguably the county's finest
surviving 19th-century gardens.*

Plate 41: Acton Reynald. One of the extraordinary octagonal flower beds, part of the scheme of about 1840.

Plate 42: Pell Wall, the rustick summerhouse. It may be as early as the 1820s, and part of the original layout of the grounds.

The new movement saw perhaps its most extravagant expression where gardens were laid out as settings for houses being built from the 1820s in the Italianate manner. Fundamental to that style were terraces, combined with the use of gravel instead of grass, statues, and evergreens, with clipped Portuguese laurels instead of orange trees. The leading proponent of the style was Charles Barry, who had travelled widely in Europe after the end of the Napoleonic Wars and had studied the Renaissance gardens of Italy. At Trentham (Staffordshire), for example, he remodelled the house in an Italianate style in 1833 and began work on the gardens in 1840, excavating two great shallow terraces between the house and the lake which he adorned with balustrades and a cast of Cellini's *Perseus*. A gondolier plied the lake, perhaps over-egging the Italian pudding. Oteley, overlooking the Mere at Ellesmere, is Shropshire's most spectacular example of such a garden, and as it is known that much of the garden was laid out by 1835[11] it must be ranked among the country's earliest (Plates 39-40).[12] The gardens were reputedly designed by Oteley's owner, Charles Kynaston Mainwaring, a keen amateur gardener, following a trip to Italy soon after his marriage in 1832. Their sheer scale and complexity, however, indicates the likelihood of professional assistance and it may be that this was provided, at least in part, by W.S. Gilpin, who published a favourable description of Oteley's grounds in 1835.[13] From the formal gardens of the house (demolished about 1960) a broad central axis descended via several flights of steps to the roof of a boathouse overlooking the mere. Off to either side of this ran four broad terraces, balustraded and buttressed in stone, one of the upper terraces being terminated with a belvidere looking down and across the garden flights. Throughout the terracing as well as elsewhere in the garden the path surfaces were of black and white decorative pebble work on a grand scale. Another Italian touch was providedby the use of large urns or 'tazzas' (from the Italian for cup), in 1851 planted with scarlet geraniums. From the terraces paths ran off to other areas of the pleasure grounds: to lawns with specimen trees including a Giant sequoia, to a Swiss cottage (present by 1851) which in 1891 stood in the centre of the '"bog garden", laid out in an old-fashioned style, like a rockery with large stones.' Other buildings include a very Italian looking campanile-style tower of about 1855, perhaps the 'observatory' mentioned in 1883.

As at Oteley, it was reputedly a honeymoon tour to Italy which produced the inspiration to create an Italian garden at Berwick, north of Shrewsbury.[14] Again, the design was said to be the work of the owner, James Watson, Conservative M.P. for Shrewsbury and 'a fine example of a self-made man' who purchased the estate in 1875 - or to be more precise his wife. The main element before the main, south, front of the house was a rectangular, sunken garden with geometric parterre and a central sundial, all enclosed within low brick walls with apsidal projections for seats midway along the long sides. *The Gardeners' Chronicle*, which carried an extensive report on the garden in 1890,[15] was especially taken with Mrs. Watson's planting scheme, which employed alpines and herbaceous plants instead of the usual 'glaring bedding plants'. Of the same date is a flight of four terraces which drops from the house down to the River Severn, the lowest faced with a red brick colonnade with 'shady recesses' for seats. Italianesque influences were also to the fore when Moor Park, near Ludlow, was modernized after its purchase in 1873 by J.J. Foster, a Yorkshire textile manufacturer.[16] Here a clear distinction was made between the informal landscape of sinuous shrubbery walks, summerhouses and a pinetum which separated the grounds from the park, and the gardens around the house. These were rigidly formal, with terraced lawns, flower beds and a fountain all confined and delimited by low retaining walls with terracotta balusters.

Other owners, architects, and garden designers preferred other influences, dominant among which, certainly architecturally, during the 1830s became the various forms of Elizabethan and Jacobean work. The leading designer of gardens in a complementary style, employing low box hedging and coloured 'gravels' - crushed brick, slate, spar, clinker and coal dust - in parterres of great complexity, was William Andrews Nesfield (d. 1881). His career took off after critical praise for his scheme for Worsley Hall (Cheshire), despite grumblings from some quarters about how little room there was in his gardens for flower beds (which rather missed the point). Other features used by Nesfield included bowling greens, mazes and arboreta, the transition from house to garden generally being via a terrace or through a geometric lawn studded with regularly spaced trees. During his career he was commissioned to undertake a large number of prestigious schemes, for instance in London at the Royal Botanic Gardens, Kew, and for the Royal Horticultural Society's garden at Kensington, although Queen Victoria rejected his proposals to lay out the entrance forecourt at Buckingham Palace with parterre and fountain. Similarly unexecuted, apparently, was a major design which he produced in 1865 for Willey Park, with elaborate formal gardens around three sides of the house including a complex parterre in front of the conservatory and a terraced walk above Willey Pools.[17] Within ten years of his death, however, there was something of a general reaction against his geometric schemes and use of gravels and owners began to do away with his parterres, planting over them or putting them down to grass. Surviving examples of his work, such as Holkham Hall (Norfolk) and Broughton Hall (North Yorkshire), are now very rare indeed.

As has already been observed, it is perhaps not helpful to be too dogmatic about particular styles. As ever, most gardens were laid out or adapted by provincial designers, or by the owners themselves, and what most looked for was a garden which was up-to-date yet at the same time fitted the house and left intact at least the main elements of any existing planting and certainly good specimen trees. Hence most gardens of the period, whilst being recognizably 19th-century, draw together in differing proportions elements of the new fashions in garden design, often applying them to an existing template of a house and its surrounds. At Stanley Hall,[18] for instance, in 1820 at the same time as the Shrewsbury architect John Smalman was remodelling the house for Sir Thomas John Tyrwhitt Jones in a fashionable gothick style, the old formal gardens were swept away and a landscape park created. A lost source, quoted in the 1870s by John Randall, describes how gate piers, gates, orchards, great holly hedges and 'other obstructions' were removed, presumably to throw the house open to its park which at the same time was improved and planted up with specimen trees. At Loton the house was twice remodelled in the 1830s by Thomas Jones of Chester, who in the later 1840s was also to supply the English and Welsh lodges there, both in the Tudor gothick style. It was presumably also Jones who, in 1835, designed an 80 metre long terrace along Loton's north facade and the circular, square and triangular flower beds edged with fat, roll-topped ceramic edging tiles which run along it.[19] A more ambitious scheme, but one where again prominently edged and geometrically shaped flower beds were an important element, was carried out at Acton Reynald in the years around 1840 as the Hall was enlarged and the grounds re-ordered for Sir Andrew Corbet.[20] Here a great flight of low terraces was created up the long west side of the Hall with a central axial path which leads past rectangular and octagonal beds and up flights of steps to a more private area screened by a yew hedge (Plate 41). This was divided into two large sunken gardens, probably formally laid out either as parterre or rose gardens, overlooked by two stone pavilions, built in 1847 against the outside of the tall, kitchen garden wall, stuccoed to blend in with the new building. The most notable features of the gardens at Acton Reynald, and which give them something of an Alice in Wonderland feel (although predating Carroll's book by 25 years), are the stone fleur-de-lis which stand sentinel at the sides of the steps and elsewhere, and the stumpy octagonal columns which rise from the corners of the octagonal flower beds. The final flourish was provided by a massive and elaborately carved stone tazza set in front of the south front of the Hall, the receptacle for spectacular summer displays of bedding plants.

The designer of the gardens at Acton Reynald has yet to be discovered, and that is true of the majority of even the more substantial Victorian gardens in Shropshire. Did Sir John Soane have

Fig. 54:
Condover Hall
about 1860, showing
the combined use
of clipped yews, urns,
and massed bedding.

any hand, for instance, in the laying out of the very fine ornamental grounds of Pell Wall, the house on the outskirts of Market Drayton which he designed in the 1820s? Those grounds include, incidentally, a splendid rustic summerhouse (Plate 42), with ling covered walls, wooden roller blinds for the door and windows, and built-in nut wood furniture, which may well be of the 1820s. Who in the 1840s laid out the intricate scrollwork parterre at Aldenham, and who about 1850[21] designed the new gardens in 17th-century style at Condover Hall? In the latter case great use was made both of yews, with the Irish variety being used to flank diamond-shaped beds with massed bedding,[22] and of box, which defines eight diagonally-divided squares containing yews clipped as pillars or cones. Below the main, garden, front of the Hall the existing, perhaps 17th-century, balustraded terracing was re-emphasised by the planting of yews and by the construction at one end of a bastion garden house and at the other of an exedra.

In the mid 19th century widely differing opinions came to be held about the layout and design of flower beds, not least because it was impossible to know what was historically appropriate to plant next to a new house designed along late medieval or Tudor lines. Some experimented with increasingly elaborate schemes embracing stars and garters, heart and tongue, and kidney-shaped beds. Elsewhere, including at Dudmaston, and probably beginning at Trentham in the 1850s, 'ribbon beds' were the favoured form, sometimes serpentine but in formal gardens straight and serving as the equivalent of herbaceous borders. The 1850s also saw the appearance of raised beds and the massing of taller plants towards the centre of the bed to give shape and interest. Photographs of the formal gardens of Sundorne castle, near Shrewsbury, taken in the later 19th century, show wigwam-like frameworks in the centre of the beds being used for support. Some took the tendency towards maximum visual impact and what has been called 'massiveness' to extremes, with huge beds laid out in strong primary colours, or using white as a base colour with blue and red.[23] Perhaps the most extensive, and certainly among the most celebrated gardens where bedding predominated was Lilleshall, laid out about 1839 (Plate 43). Here, alongside the 'Duchess's rose garden', a 570-foot long apple walk or pergola, and grass terraces, were both circular and ribbon beds, where in 1898 it was said 'the blaze of colour is attained by boldly contrasting various hues to secure rich effect, dark colours are opposed to light; zonal pelargoniums, calceolarias, and tuberous begonias being amongst the most important plants used.'[24]

Fig. 55:
The Druid Oaks in Oakly Park,
photographed in the later 19th century.

Another garden where the bedding was an essential element of a formal layout was that at Apley Park, near Bridgnorth, which in 1867 was bought from the Whitmores by W.O. Foster, the proprietor of the nearby Apleyforge ironworks.[25] He brought in Edward Milner, one of the leading landscape designers of the times, whose main contribution was to rescarp the steeply sloping ground south of the house to create a more dramatic setting. Below and to either side of the terracing the landscaping was more varied with yew hedging, an exedra (or apse), and a massive fountain, with the formality being relieved around the edges of the garden by specimen trees. Probably also part of the overall design was a 'waterfall rockery' to one side of the terracing, a typical touch designed to suggest the history of geological development, one of Milner's favourite themes.

Throughout the period landscape parks continued to be seen as the only appropriate setting for a country house, to be grazed, wherever possible, by deer. In the early 1720s Burford House, near Tenbury Wells, was bought by William Bowles, proprietor of the Vauxhall glass works. By such a purchase Bowles was making the classic move into landed society, and much of the attraction of the estate was presumably the deer park it was advertized to include. Six years litigation followed Bowles's discovery that on at least this point he had been duped.[26] In the mid 19th century the creation of a 70 acre deer park, along with a museum wing on the house, were among T.C. Eyton's improvements at Eyton upon the Weald Moors. On his death in 1880 its herd of fallow deer was sold to the earl of Derby to augment his herd at Knowsley.[27] Such movements of stock, whether through a sale or by gift, had been common since the Middle Ages, and about 1800, for instance, deer were sent from Aldenham to restock Attingham park. An unusual building associated with the management of deer is the deer house in Ludford park, near Ludlow, a circular, stone building externally resembling a dovecote, within which the deer would be driven for shelter in especially hard weather (Plate 44). Its date is unknown, but it may well be of the later 18th or early 19th century.[28]

One of the most extraordinary attempts to diversify a park's stock took place at Hawkstone, where in the 1850s Viscount Hill introduced the eland, a South African antelope, which was vigorously promoted as a meat producing animal.[29] Hill was not alone in seeking its acclimatization, and in 1860 a widely reported 'eland dinner' was held in London where a roast joint of the beast was consumed and pronounced the most 'masticable of any meat ... *mammalian* meat with a soupcon of pheasant flavour.' Following the success of the dinner an Acclimatisation Society, with Hill among its patrons, was formed to promote its introduction along with an improbable range of other plants and animals. It was confidently predicted that the near future would see 'troops of elands gracefully galloping over our green sward', and that by the end of the century it would be established as a 'solid and useful' farm animal. In the event, despite a flurry of activity in its early years and some of the most

Fig. 56:
Pell Wall, Sir John Soane's
Triangular Lodge.

incredible feasts ever seen with kangaroo, Chinese lamb, and Japanese sea-slug all on the menu, the society foundered in 1868.[30] How long the Hawkstone eland herd survived it for the moment remains unknown.

As earlier, park lodges provided ideal opportunities for essays in miniature on architecture, and on increasingly whimsical themes.[31] Some designers adopted a rustick or Swiss style, as at Pontesford House about 1830, although the most popular vocabulary continued to be 'minimalist-Classical', as used in the 1820s by C.R. Cockerell at Oakly, and by the Shrewsbury architect Edward Haycock at Onslow in the later 1820s and for Hope Dale lodge at Millichope Park about twenty years later.[32] Perhaps most notable architecturally is Sir John Soane's remarkable triangular lodge at Pell Wall of the 1820s; here there is only a hint of neo-Classical survival, and instead an employment of almost pure geometric triangular forms. Later in the century a more neo-vernacular style became popular with timber-framed upper storeys, low eaves and fretted bargeboards, a style adopted about 1870 for the lodge to Norman Shaw's Preen Manor and in the 1890s by Aston Webb for the lodges to Yeaton Peverey.[33] Even so, it was far from universal. In the 1880s Shaw (or perhaps W.R. Lethaby; an exact attribution has yet to be made),[34] in a very early use of the style, used the neo-Georgian for the pair of Tittenly lodges at Shavington, while about 1870 at Ludstone Hall and in 1890 at Stokesay Court it was the Jacobean period which provided the inspiration. Finally, about 1904, an Arts and Crafts style was used for the new lodges at Ruckley Grange near Shifnal by the London architects employed to rebuild Ruckley by new owner Thomas Reid Walker, a Burton-upon-Trent brewer.[35]

Towards the end of the 18th century and especially in the early 19th century more and more gentry houses were built around the edges of towns like Shrewsbury. Such residences, most of them more villa than country house, allowed their owners to participate in the benefits of urban life and, if in 'trade' to keep an eye on business, while at the same time enjoying a modest reflection of the traditional aristocratic rural lifestyle. Many affected a park, with five or ten acres around the house put down to pasture and dotted with specimen trees, but few ventured to more ambitious features. Hadley Hall, near Wellington, bought in 1848 by the Wolverhampton ironmaster G.B. Thorneycroft and renamed Hadley Park, provides a good example.[36] One exception was at Copthorne, on the west side of Shrewsbury, where in the later 18th century the powerful north Welsh land agent and surveyor John Probert built a new brick house behind which lay pleasure grounds and a small park. Those included wooded walks; a small lake with several arms, perhaps contrived from excavations for marl, with a boathouse and two rustic bridges; a Swiss cottage; and a grotto, which when the house's contents were sold in 1827 contained eight painted chairs. Copthorne also had a walled kitchen garden, its tools and equipment including a glass frame, six bell glasses, ladders, a spade, mattock, two 'scuffles' (hoes), three rakes, a stone roller and large numbers of flower and shrub pots, fifty of them containing 'green house plants and flowers.'[37]

Another of Shrewsbury's town edge gardens was that of The Mount, home of Dr. Robert Waring Darwin (Plate 45): physician, successful property speculator, husband of Josiah Wedgewood's daughter Susannah, and father of the naturalist Charles. The family's interest in botany and gardening was well established before Charles's birth in 1809, his grandfather Erasmus having published a scientific poem *The Botanic Garden* in 1791 and his great-uncle a botanic textbook. His growing wealth during the early 19th century enabled Dr. Darwin to create at the Mount a garden full of exotic rarities, some of which, including the white flowered 'fly-catcher' and the ornamental opium poppy, were inherited from his father's collection while others were collected or purchased. Tender specimens were kept in a hothouse which lead off the morning room, 'an exotic indoor jungle' which presumably housed many of the plants listed when the contents of the Mount were dispersed in 1866 including nine large orange trees in pots, azaleas, camelias, ferns, and specimen primulas. The young Charles rapidly gained an intimate knowledge of the garden, not least by helping his father with a garden book, modelled on Gilbert White's *Selborne*, in which a day-by-day record was kept of weather, temperature, first flowerings and fruitings. 'Papa asked me to do this', notes one entry. 'Ther was in year 1819, 160 flower on the Poenies [Peonies]. In the year 1820, 384 flower. In the year 1821, 363 flower.'[38]

Among the suppliers of exotic trees and shrubs to Shrewsbury gentleman was William Cobbett, today best remembered as a radical social commentator and author of the *Rural Rides* (1830), but from 1819 a professional nurseryman specialising in American species, with which he had become acquainted during ten years in the United States. In 1827, and presumably from Cobbett's first printed *Catalogue of American Trees, Shrubs and Seeds for Sale,*[39] John Watton (d.1850), proprietor and editor of *Eddowses Salopian Journal*, ordered various items for his garden, which was probably somewhere behind the *Journal* office in St. John's Hill.[40] The order was despatched in early March, but was incomplete, as a letter from Cobbett explained. 'I have only been able to send you two Iron Woods, no Tulip, Gum or Locust trees, these having been all sold or all destroyed by the late frosts. I hope, however, my preparations for the next fall will enable me to supply every gentleman who may honour me with their commands.'[41]

A contemporary Shrewsbury garden of a very different character was that of Archdeacon Hugh Owen, the town's historian, in Swan Hill.[42] Here Owen constructed a summerhouse embellished inside and out with carved stone and woodwork, stained glass and other pieces of what we would

Fig. 57:
A more typical lodge,
at the entrance to Willey Park.

today term architectural salvage, rescued from buildings in Shrewsbury and beyond including St. Chad's and St. Alkmund's churches as they were demolished or gutted. Other pieces seem to have been used in a rockery and in general garden adornment.

Another town-edge gentleman's house was The Quinta, north of Oswestry, rebuilt in the later 1850s for Thomas Barnes M.P.[43] Even for the times it is a remarkably unattractive house, in a dull grey limestone. Its one saving grace was that it lay within a park, established by Frederick West, from whom Barnes had bought the Quinta, in the 1830s. In that park, in a slight declivity on the edge of what became Temple Wood, West had built, probably in the mid 1840s, what is one of the most eccentric park structures in Shropshire, a half-scale Stonehenge (Plate 46). The stones, however, were raised exactly as quarried from Llanymynech, undressed and with the holes for explosive charges still visible down their edges. But even if the air is of a hurried project done on the cheap, the result is rather fun, and a worthy addition to the small group of Shropshire park features - the Druid's seat at Hopton Court and the stone circle at The Nursery, West Felton - with an antiquarian inspiration.

Among the iron masters' houses around the Ironbridge Gorge was 'Sunniside', built about 1750 at the top of Coalbrookdale by Abraham Darby II.[44] By the early 19th century it had been provided with ornamental grounds said by one visitor to be of 'great taste and ingenuity', with 'hot house and green house with a good collection of plants native and exotic, also a bath and summerhouse'. Although a herd of deer was kept at Sunniside[45] (Fig. 71) for much of the 19th century it would have been hard for the Darbys to claim it as a park, and indeed the same anonymous visitor in his description of Sunniside's surrounds while at first describing them as a 'park and fine sheet of water' then crossed that out and substituted 'paddock and fish pond'.[46]

Sunniside looked west across Coalbrookdale to the Workmen's Walks, laid out in the later 18th century by Abraham Darby II's son-in-law Richard Reynolds. In the earlier 19th one or two other walks were provided by philanthropists as ideas about public health reforms took root, especially after publication of the report by the Select Committee on Public Walks (1833). This important document, presaging fifty years of legislative provision enabling the development of public parks, enshrined the principle of 'open space' and looked at how the working class family could be provided with proper, and sober, means of recreation. One of the key movers of that report was R.A. Slaney, M.P., of Hatton Grange, a consistent champion of means to improve the lot of both

Fig. 58:
R. A. Stanley, M.P.,
champion of open spaces for the poor.

Fig. 59:
Nancy Spragge, provider of teas
on Haughmond Hill.

the urban and the rural poor.[47] Slaney's particular enthusiasm was public walks, and on his own estate he gave three acres of land on the summit of Brimstree Hill as a public walk and built a stone summerhouse there where 'conveniences' were provided and where hot water could be got for tea.[48] Other landowners may have been similarly influenced to offer encouragement to temperate visitors wishing to climb vantage points on their land. Nescliffe Hill, for instance, became much frequented on Sundays and holidays; hot water was dispensed in an area called the 'tea tents', and until damaged by vandals about 1900 there was reputedly a maze.[49] Haughmond Hill, near Shrewsbury, where tea was provided by Nancy Spragge,[50] was also popular, as was the Wrekin near Wellington.

In a number of instances landowners actually opened their own gardens to visitors on a regular basis. In 1854 R.A. Slaney was reported[51] to have again, as for several years past, opened Walford Manor gardens to his tenants for a Cottage Fete of which the highlight was the 'Walford Games', a mixture of athletics and rustic sports. At Ellesmere Cremorne Gardens - named, presumably ironically, after the notorious London commercial pleasure grounds of that name - were laid out in the mid 19th century adjoining Ellesmere House, the Shropshire residence of Earl Brownlow. They ran from the house, round the Mere to Crimps Field, and were planted with a wide variety of trees and shrubs and provided with tennis courts, a summerhouse, boat house and lawns. On certain days and when the earl and his family were not in residence the gardens were open to the 'better sort' among the public; parties from Merseyside and Staffordshire required written permission to enter, and had to undertake only to play 'controlled' games.[52] By the 1850s Badger Dingle, too, was being opened to all comers on bank holidays, many of those visitors later coming in charabanc parties from the Black Country.

In at least one case, at Hodge Bower in Ironbridge, pleasure grounds were opened as a commercial proposition. Here the proprietor was Thomas Wilson, the landlord of the *Crown Inn*, who hoped his facilities would replace those of the recently closed Enville Gardens in Staffordshire, making Ironbridge a 'principal summer resort' of the 'toiling masses of the Black Country' and Hodge Bower the 'Brighton of the Midland counties.' In the later 1870s parties of up to 350 would visit the pleasure grounds, taking refreshment there and enjoying the view (a powerful telescope was provided) before going on to visit one of the local industrial concerns, or scenic ruins, or to search for geological specimens.[53]

*Plate 43: The blazing colours of Lilleshall, in an early 20th-century picture.
The view looks over the roof of Wyatville's orangery of the late 1820s.*

Plate 44: A deer house in Ludford Park, near Ludlow.
The park was present by 1752, and this structure, designed to shelter its deer,
is perhaps of later 18th- or 19th-century date.

*Plate 45: Dr. Robert Darwin, medical man, property speculator,
and father of Charles. In the early 19th century
his was probably Shrewsbury's finest garden.*

Plate 46: The half-scale Stonehenge, built near The Quinta
in the 1840s. It is a less than precise replica.

Plate 47: The glasshouses in the kitchen gardens at Millichope Park.
Great curvilinear structures like these were popular
in the third quarter of the 19th century.

Fig. 60:
Shrewsbury's
Quarry in the late
19th century.

By then, however, there was a declining need for the philanthropic or commercial provision of open space and amusement, as from the later 1840s, as a direct consequence of the work of Slaney and his fellow public health campaigners, a series of Acts was passed enabling the provision of recreation grounds and municipal parks.[54] At first principally places for fresh air and 'rational recreation' (rather than the traditional rowdier kind, such as the Wrekin wakes which usually ended with a battle on the Wrekin)[55] they became in the last quarter of the century one of the main expressions of civic pride, with gates, benches and bandstands all vying for space among beds of regimented bedding plants. In Shropshire the movement is best characterized by what happened in Shrewsbury, where in the later 1870s the Corporation acquired the Quarry and made it available to the Shropshire Horticultural Society for its annual exhibition. Once established at the Quarry the

Fig. 61:
Coalbrookdale garden benches
from the 1875 catalogue.
Top is 'Boys and Griffiths',
with 'Osmunda Fern' below.
The latter was available bronzed,
or painted green or chocolate,
and both were offered with
iron, pine or oak seats.

latter body began to give regular and generous sums for its improvement, providing a bandstand (1879), gates (early 1880s), and a new lodge (1885), as well as funding projects to clean out and plant the Dingle and to plant new avenues. Another relatively early piece of municipal improvement took place in Bridgnorth, where in 1869 the Corporation paid for what appear to have previously been four allotments to be planted with shrubs in order to enhance the Castle Walks.[56]

One of the principal suppliers of ornamental ironwork for parks and gardens was the Coalbrookdale Company, and from the 1830s it appears that a wide range of garden furniture was being manufactured in its foundry near Ironbridge.[57] Only in 1875, however, did the firm issue a comprehensive catalogue of those goods: an astonishing record of Victorian taste and ingenuity as well as of the company's diverse range of products.[58] Most spectacular perhaps were the cast iron fountains, which ranged from boys entwined with a serpent or swan, or a figure from ancient Egypt, to a clump of bullrushes. If so desired these could be combined in a spouting aquatic tableau with boys and swans gambolling among bullrushes and conch blowing mermaids. Fountains could be supplied either painted or bronzed as could statues, vases, and for the parlour or conservatory flower stands and jardinieres. Perhaps best known are the benches and garden chairs, now highly valued, which were available in many styles, including Gothic, Elizabethan, Italian, and Rustic, or featuring figurative medallions depicting 'A Midsummer Night's Dream', or 'Boys and Griffins'. Then as now, however, the more popular lines seem to have featured seats contrived from vines, branches and leaves, often in verdant abundance, the 1875 catalogue illustrating, among others, the 'Nasturtium', 'Fern and Blackberry', 'Oak and Ivy', 'Water Plant', 'Lily of the Valley', and 'Osmunda Fern' designs. The catalogue urged customers to order benches, chairs, and garden rollers 'as early in the year as possible, in order that they be ready for delivery in March and April.'

The same movement which produced improved recreation facilities in towns also had an effect in the countryside, and the General Enclosure Act of 1845 empowered the Inclosure Commissioners to set aside land for recreation when commons and wastes were inclosed.[59] Admittedly provision was often modest, and in Shropshire when 8,208 acres of Clun Forest were inclosed in 1847, besides the allotment of plots for schools, a chapel and a curate's house, just one acre was set aside as a recreation ground, on a hill top above Newcastle. In 1876 legislation required a more generous provision, but only one Shropshire parish benefitted. That was Llanfair, where allotments made in 1891 when 1,634 of the Llanfair hills were inclosed included 15 acres for labourers' 'field gardens' and 10 acres as a recreation ground, the same Award also preserving the 1 1/2-mile stretch of Offa's Dyke that passed through the newly-inclosed land as a public footpath.[60]

Decent gardens also formed a key element of most model cottages built by improving 19th-century landlords, although the number of those in Shropshire was never large; their number included Lord Craven on the Stokesay estate, Sir Rowland Hill of Hawkstone, and Sir Baldwin Leighton of Loton Park. Decent housing and the provision of gardens or allotments was intended by such men to encourage a sober and provident labour force. Another inducement to such behaviour was the cottage garden societies which grew up, usually through the patronage of a landlord or parson, in the mid 19th century. The Morfe Cottage Garden Society was founded in 1847, and in 1848 its annual show in the grounds of Apley Park drew a reputed 5-6,000 guests.[61] Bromfield too had a society by then,[62] Walford's was founded about 1860,[63] and undoubtedly there were many others. The scale of Prees Horticultural Society's show, first held in 1863 and under the patronage of the Hills, shows how important such events became in the annual round, with dozens of cash prizes. In the1860s prizes were offered for the finest pig and the best cultivated garden among cottages with an annual rental of under £10, although by the mid 1870s those categories had been dropped and the emphasis was solely on vegetables, flowers and fruits.[64]

PRIZES.

POTATOES.

	s.	d.
For the best twelve Winter ...	5	0
„ Second best ditto ...	2	6
„ Third best ditto ...	1	6
For the best twelve Seconds...	5	0
„ Second best ditto ...	2	6
„ Third best ditto ...	1	6
For the best twelve Early ...	5	0
„ Second best ditto ...	2	6
„ Third best ditto ...	1	6

CARROTS.
(To be Tailed and Cleaned but not Topped.)

	s.	d.
For the best six Red ...	2	6
„ Second best ditto ...	1	6
„ Third best ditto ...	1	0
For the best six White ...	2	6
„ Second best ditto ...	1	6
„ Third best ditto ..	1	0

PARSNIPS.
(To be Tailed and Cleaned but not Topped.)

	s.	d.
For the best six ...	2	6
„ Second best ditto ...	1	6

TURNIPS.
(To be Cleaned and Tailed but not Topped.)

	s.	d.
For the best six White ...	2	6
„ Second best ditto ...	1	6
„ Third best ditto ...	1	0
For the best six yellow ...	2	6
„ Second best ditto ...	1	6
„ Third best ditto ...	1	0

ONIONS.

	s.	d.
For the best twelve ...	5	0
„ Second best ditto ...	3	0
„ Third best ditto ...	2	0
„ Fourth ditto ...	1	6

SHALLOTS.

	s.	d.
For the best twelve ..	2	6
„ Second best ditto ..	1	6

CABBAGES.

	s.	d.
For the best three White ...	3	0
„ Second best ditto ...	1	6
For the best three Red ...	3	0
„ Second best ditto ...	1	6
For the best three Ox Cabbages	3	0
„ Second best ditto ...	1	6

GREENS.

	s.	d.
For the best four	2	6
„ Second best ditto ...	1	6

CAULIFLOWERS.

	s.	d.
For the best three ...	2	6
„ Second best ditto ...	1	6

HERBS.

	s.	d.
For the best bunch	2	6
„ Second best ditto ...	1	6

CUCUMBERS.

	s.	d.
For the best ditto	2	6
„ Second best ditto ...	1	6

VEGETABLE MARROWS.

	s.	d.
For the best two	2	6
„ Second best ditto ..	1	6

PEAS.

	s.	d.
For the best quart in pods ...	5	0
„ Second best ditto ...	2	6

BEANS.

	s.	d.
For the best quart Scarlet Runners	2	6
„ Second best ditto ...	1	6

CELERY.

	s.	d.
For the best three sticks White	2	6
„ Second best ditto ...	1	6
„ Third best ditto ...	1	0
For the best three sticks Red	2	6
„ Second best ditto ...	1	6
„ Third best ditto ...	1	0

MANGOLD WURTZEL.
(To be Tailed and Cleaned but not Topped.)

	s.	d.
For the best six	3	6
„ Second best ditto ...	2	6
„ Third best ditto ...	2	0

FRUITS.

	s.	d.
For the best six Eating Pears	5	0
„ Second best ditto ...	2	6
For the best six Baking Pears	5	0
„ Second best ditto ...	2	6
For the best six Eating Apples	5	0
„ Second best ditto ...	2	6
„ Third best ditto ...	1	6
For the best six Baking Apples	5	0
„ Second best ditto ...	2	6
„ Third best ditto ...	1	6
For the best quart of Damsons	2	6
„ Second best ditto ...	1	6
For the best twelve Plums of any sort	5	0
„ Second best ditto ...	2	6
For the best pound of Filberts	2	6
„ Second best ditto ...	1	6
For the best pound of any other Nuts	2	6
„ Second best ditto ...	1	6

FLOWERS.

	s.	d.
For the best six Dahalias ...	2	6
„ Second best ditto ...	1	6
For the best six Hollyhocks ...	2	6
„ Second best ditto ...	1	6
For the best six Roses ...	2	6
„ Second best ditto ...	1	6
For the best Fushia in Pot ...	2	6
„ Second best ditto ...	1	6
For the best twelve Pansies		
„ Second best ditto ...	1	6
For the best twelve Stocks ...	3	0
„ Second best ditto ...	1	6
For the best twelve Asters ...	3	0
„ Second best ditto ...	1	6
For the best cut Nosegay of Garden Flowers... ...	5	0
„ Second best ditto ...	2	6
For the best cut Nosegay of Wild Flowers (grown in Prees)	5	0
„ Second best ditto ...	2	6

The SHOW will be opened at Two o'clock p. m., and will close at Six. Admission : One Shilling each from Two till Three o'clock ; Sixpence each from Three to Four o'clock, afterwards, Threepence each. Children under 14 years. of age admitted at Five o'clock at one Halfpenny each. Candidates for the Prizes are required to give one week's notice to the Secretary. COLONEL FREDERIC HILL, of Prees Hall, has kindly undertaken to present the Prizes at Five o'clock.

JOHN MORRIS, PRINTER, WYLE COP, SHREWSBURY.

Fig. 62: Poster advertizing the cottage gardeners' show at Prees, 1874.

Fig. 63:
The immaculate
kitchen garden
at Pell Wall,
photographed
in 1911.

Aside from parks there were a number of other improvements in the mid 19th century designed to enhance the appearance of towns. In 1852 several gentlemen combined to purchase the castle mound at Oswestry, which was then fenced in and an arboretum begun. Access was restricted to five-shilling subscribers.[65] In Albrighton lime trees were planted along the High Street about 1850 by Oson Bidwell, the bailiff,[66] and twenty or thirty years later similar schemes were implemented in the Square in Shrewsbury and in Barrow Street, Much Wenlock.[67] Cemeteries, too, especially municipal ones such as Ellesmere's of the 1860s, were increasingly well ordered, and many were laid out almost as gardens for the dead, with ornamental planting, walks, and seats.

Similarly, from the 1840s there was a much greater emphasis given to the setting of public buildings and institutions. At Shrewsbury the County Asylum, opened in 1845, was provided with eleven acres of grounds, said in 1851 to be 'laid out with admirable taste and cultivated by the patients.' Around the kitchen gardens, which supplied it with food, was a terrace where the female patients were allowed to walk.[68] The movement was perhaps most pronounced in the educational world, at least insofar as the private sector was concerned, and the advertisements of the growing band of 'public' schools tended to make much of the sporting facilities, and good air, available to their students.

One of the main advances in gardening in the early years of Victoria's reign came as the cost of glass fell sharply. Technical developments, notably the invention of sheet glass in 1833, made possible the manufacture of bigger panes of glass, and after the removal of glass tax in 1845 and the repeal of window tax in 1851 there was a boom in both conservatory and greenhouse construction (Plate 47). Glasshouses with ever more specialized functions proliferated, and by the later 19th century the larger establishments in the county would probably have houses for grapes, peaches, melons and cucumbers, bananas and pineapples, figs and nectarines, cherries and plums, ferns, azaleas, hyacinths and orchids. One of the most impressive and well laid out sets of greenhouses in the county was that built about 1870 at Pell Wall, where the kitchen garden with integral gardener's house formed part of Sir John Soane's original design of the 1820s. Within the garden itself were tall, curvilinear glasshouses, at least partly given over to vines, while outside, in a holly hedged enclosure, were ranges of freestanding glasshouses of a similar but lower design, some of them with basements dug in to the ground, where such things as cucumbers and chrysanthemums were grown. Of perhaps much the same date was the tall, apsidal conservatory built on to the south side of the house containing a fountain and billiard room and with a forcing loft above.[69]

Glass was also used extensively in the grounds of Benthall Hall, home between 1853 and 1886 of George Maw, the leading manufacturer of ceramic tiles.[70] Despite his involvement, with his brother Arthur, in the development of one of the largest factories in the Ironbridge Gorge, he still found the time to spend long periods abroad in the 1850s and 1860s collecting plants in the mountainous areas around the Mediterranean. Most of Maw's collection was of alpines, which although tolerant of the cold of English winters were less so of rain, sleet and melting snow, and so in order to provide protection Maw had dug a large, curved ditch, 30 yards long, 10 feet wide and 3 feet deep, with brick-lined sides and hinged glass frames to cover it. By 1870 the garden at Benthall contained 3-4,000 distinct species, identified with colour-coded clay labels manufactured at Maw's own works: black ones were used to mark plants from which seeds were to be collected, blue for those off which cuttings were to be taken, and yellow for species to be dried for the herbarium. Maw's researches culminated in 1886 with the publication of *A Monograph of the Genus Crocus*, a lavishly illustrated and highly acclaimed work of scholarship on crocuses.

At many other houses, such as Apley Park, and Leaton Knolls where the large and south-facing gardens with integral gardener's house were under construction in 1851, the proliferation of glasshouses heralded a period of investment in the kitchen gardens which ushered in a golden age. The range and quality of its flowers, vegetables and especially fruit became, more than ever before, one of the key indicators of a household's status. As early as 1796 a high point of the newspaper report on the visit of the Prince and Princess of Orange to Hawkstone was the description of the

Fig. 64: Diddlesbury Hall. A photograph taken about 1900 to mark the completion of the extraordinary palm house.

*Fig. 65:
A late 19th-century
photograph of the
gardeners - and
presumably the cook -
at Acton Reynald,
posed in front of the
Temple in the
Ladies' Walk.*

two bunches of grapes which adorned the table, one weighing sixteen pounds and the other eleven.[71]
Few, however, would have enjoyed a garden's bounty with quite the abandon of the young
Charles Darwin. In 1828, while home from Cambridge for the holidays, he became a frequent
visitor to Woodhouse, near Oswestry, where he was courting Fanny Owen. It was the strawberry
season, and Woodhouse's beds were full of the luscious fruit, forming a 'perfect stalking ground.'
He and Fanny first got down on their hands and knees and then lower still, until they were
stretched out 'full length' beside each other, 'grazing' the berries and behaving like beasts.[72]
Outsize vegetables even became a matter of public interest, and in 1842 'T.E.' of Shrewsbury wrote
to the *Salopian Phoenix* to report the cultivation at Pitchford by a 'young gentleman ... well known for
his superior skill in Horticulture' of an extraordinary cucumber, 2 lbs. 11 oz. in weight and with an
extreme length 'being a little curved' of 24 1/8 inches.[73]

Milner, Jekyll and Page: 1880 onwards

As always, much of the investment in new houses and gardens in the later 19th century was by industrialists whose business interests lay outside Shropshire. Between 1869 and 1874, for instance, J.D. Allcroft, a successful Worcester glover, put together by purchase a 6,000 acre estate centred on a modest country house called Stonehouse, in Onibury.[1] In 1889 that was replaced by Stokesay Court, an 88-room Elizabethan-style mansion designed by Thomas Harris, the first person to use the term 'Victorian architecture' and the architect of several other country houses in Shropshire. Also part of Harris's contract were the stables, lodge, drive and bridge, and the extensive brick-walled kitchen gardens and hothouses. The pleasure grounds, however, were set out to a scheme supplied in 1892 by one of the country's leading designers Henry Ernest Milner. Here Milner was fortunate in having a mature landscape with a series of valley bottom pools to work around, and his main contribution seems to have been to create a serpentine network of paths which wound across the front lawn and down to the pools, with terracotta vases and a fountain. He may also have embellished what is one of the most attractive features surviving from Stonehouse's gardens, a sunken quarry or rock garden with a dripping well, probably created in the early 19th century. Milner's bill[2] was £97, a drop in the ocean compared to the £100,000 or so Allcroft laid out on his transformation of theStonehouse or the £56,000 spent on estate improvements.

Fig. 66:
A garden party
at Stokesay Court about 1930.

At Ruckley Grange, near Shifnal (Plate 48), a similar transformation was wrought by a Burton-upon-Trent brewer Thomas Reid Walker after his purchase of the estate about 1896.[3] The house itself was rebuilt to a very high standard in a neo-Elizabethan style by the London architects Sir Ernest George and Yates, who also designed new outbuildings and gardens. South of the house they created a formal garden in the Italianate style, with stone balustrading along low terraces, tall hedges of dark green yew punctuated with golden yew, and as the principal feature a long stone basin or canal with a copper-roofed summerhouse at its far end. Here was order, muted colours, even austerity, very different from the brightly coloured parterre flower gardens and the 'mazy wilderness walks' mentioned in the sale catalogue of 1895. West of the house lawns and specimen trees overlooked and ran down to Ruckley Pool, which had been enlarged and screened with ornamental woodlands in the early 19th century. Below, but out of sight of the house, an open air swimming pool was created - a notably early example of such a facility[4] - an oval stone basin 15 metres across with a Swiss chalet-style changing room. For two new park lodges, also of about 1904, a different architectural vocabulary was chosen, that of the Arts and Crafts movement. Relatively little building in this style, inspired by John Ruskin and William Morris and a reaction to Victorian mass production, took place in Shropshire, but Ruckley and Timlet lodges, with their pebble-dashed walls and tiled roofs, are fine and restrained examples.

Ruckley was not the only garden touched by the renewed Italianate influences of the late 19th century. At Pell Wall, for instance, an Italian garden was created about 1909 by its new owner J. Munroe Walker, another brewer.[5] Here the garden was created as an additional compartment leading from the Lower Pool, with a linear pond or canal with a central circular basin all manufactured in concrete. Later, when Pell Wall was occupied by the Brothers' Christian Institution (1927-1960s), the Italian garden was walled-in and converted to a swimming pool, to be completely forgotten until the gardens were restored in the 1990s by the Udall family.

Ludstone Hall, a fine moated house of about 1607 five miles east of Bridgnorth, saw restoration in the 1870s after its purchase by Joseph Round Cartwright, a recently widowed Sedgley fire-brick manufacturer.[6] Around it he created formal gardens sympathetic to the old house, with brick lodges in the Jacobean style by Robert Griffiths of Stafford, a brick bridge across the moat, and especially a knot garden contained within tall yew hedges. Here low box hedges were used to form six beds in the shape of playing card suits (Plate 49), each of four sections and with a central, spirally-clipped box tree. By now such revivalist gardens were remarkably successful and often historically accurate, and certainly that at Ludstone adds greatly to the setting of the Hall.

Another successful evocation of an historic garden was at Yeaton Peverey, a few miles north of Shrewsbury, although here it was around a new house built 1889-92 for Sir Offley Wakeman, a landowner, barrister, and chairman of Quarter Sessions. Although describing it as 'an astonishing Jacobean fantasy' Pevsner was generally dismissive of the house, designed by Aston Webb, deeming it 'much less original and truly original than Norman Shaw.'[7] Less didactic commentators, however, have found enjoyment in the mixture of olde English manorial styles put together by Webb, and especially with the terraced garden front. The landscaping, as at Stokesay Court two years later, was by H.E. Milner, whose father Edward (who had worked, probably with his son's assistance, at Apley park in the 1870s) had been a leading figure in the gardening world from the 1860s until his death in 1884. It was while at work on Yeaton, in 1890, that Henry brought out his influential book on the *Art and Practice of Landscape Gardening* , which helped establish him, in his own right, as among the leaders of his profession.[8] His father thought that everything visible from the terrace should show the hand of man, but Henry favoured a more restrained style with less formality, and at Yeaton he followed that ideal using shrubberies and specimen trees to create gardens which

*Plate 48: Ruckley Grange, where about 1900
the house and grounds were transformed by a brewer.*

*Plate 49: Ludstone Hall, the knot garden laid out
by J. R. Cartwright in the later 19th century.*

*Plate 50: The service buildings and kitchen gardens at Ludstone,
also refurbished by Cartwright.*

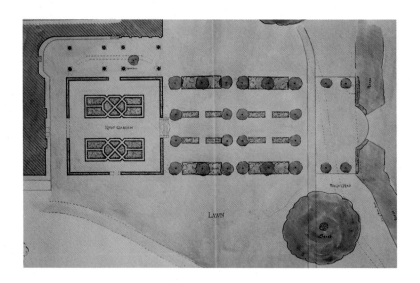

*Plate 51: Brenda Colvin's unexecuted design of 1929
for a knot garden at Attingham Hall, linking the hall with the River Severn.*

*Plate 52: The pleached limes at Chyknell, part of Russell Page's
stunning formal garden of 1951.*

*Plate 53: The yew alley at Longnor Hall,
planted about 1960.*

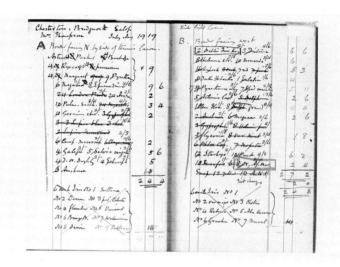

*Plate 54: Gertrude Jekyll's notebook recording
her commission at Chesterton in 1919. Seen here are two
of the six pages dealing with the job.*

*Plate 55: J. W. Coombes, Apley Park's last Head Gardener,
photographed in 1966. The glasshouses are now derelict.*

were sympathetic to the feel of the house.

Another style which enjoyed a vogue at the turn of the century was Japanese gardens.
After that country's long period of isolation from the west ended with the Meiji restoration of 1868,
knowledge of the Japanese arts gradually developed through the writings and illustrations of
European travellers. Between 1880 and 1910 (a period which saw the first performance of *The Mikado*
and *Madame Butterfly*) many Japanese gardens were created in Britain, characterized by the use of
weeping willows, Korean pines, spiraeas, azaleas and primulas around contrived Japanese-style
landscapes with lakes, pagodas, bridges, rocks and lanterns. Only one certain example has so far
been located in Shropshire, at Aston Hall near Oswestry, although little now remains there beyond
a circular depression which was the main setting for the garden and a stone pedestal.
Here the Japanese garden was present by 1890.[9]

France provided the inspiration for a grand, chateau-style house at The Grove, near Craven Arms,
built in 1878 for John Jones, a prosperous iron master and banker. It later became the home of his
daughter Harriet, whose husband, David Greene K.C., was a son of a former Governor of the Bank
of England. Under her the original modest grounds were extended to form a small park, while about
1905 the gardens were further embellished by the creation of a rose garden, lily pond and rock
garden. Ten men then worked in the gardens. Rather severe red brick and timber framed lodges on
the main Shrewsbury - Ludlow road announced the estate to passers-by.[10]

One of the best known firms of garden designers and contractors, specialising in the production of
artificial rockeries, was Pulham's. James Pulham, the son of one of the pioneers of Portland cement
manufacture, began to use cement and clinker to make rockery stones in the 1840s, and although
the firm later also used real stone and terracotta its 'Pulhamite' structures (such as those at Battersea
and Wisley) are what it is best remembered for. In Shropshire the firm was responsible for designing
a rock garden at Henley Hall, near Ludlow, where about 1900 a series of descending pools with
Pulhamite rockwork was formed together with a bank planted with yellow flowers including
dahlias, mulleins, and nasturtiums to provide a vivid contrast with dark green clipped yews and
Scots pines.[11] That was part of a wholesale reordering of the pleasure grounds undertaken at about
that time at Henley which in general made great use of straight lines and hard surfaces to produce
a landscape with a remarkably modernist feeling.[12]

A key theme in a number of gardens in the earlier 20th century was the planting of exotics.
At Sansaw, built in 1888 for J.J. Bibby, the Liverpool cattle feed and shipping magnate,[13] plaques
show how marriages, births and other family celebrations were commemorated by planting a tree.
As early as 1913, when *The Gardeners' Magazine* visited Sansaw, the Irish yews, beeches, a giant
Sequoia and a blue spruce had become noteworthy specimens.[14] Many of these are now mature,
and are key elements in the magnificent grounds. At Apley Park there was a more concentrated
period of planting, following the despatch there in 1927 by Lady Londonderry of a large number of
rhododendron collected by the botanical expeditions of Rock in 1923-4 and Kingdon-Ward in 1924-5.

Probably the largest garden created in the earlier 20th century was that at Hodnet Hall, developed
between 1921 and the 1950s by Brigadier A.G.W. Heber Percy. Here a chain of lakes and pools was
excavated, terraces formed and views opened to the landscape beyond as a setting was created for
a massive programme of planting of trees, shrubs and bulbs from all parts of the world.

Brenda Colvin (d. 1981), who was to go on to become one of the best known and influential
landscape designers of the mid 20th century, was employed at Burwarton in the 1920s to extend the

19th-century terracing. Her scheme included, on the lowest level, a rose garden within yew hedges. She was also brought in at Attingham in 1929 by Lady Berwick to produce schemes for two contrasting gardens close to the Hall: a 'wild garden' in the area now occupied by the spring garden, and on the east side of the house a knot garden with formal walks down to the river (Plate 51). In the event neither was implemented, although the plans still survive.[15] While it would be too much to claim that the mid 20th century saw a return to favour of formal gardens there were one or two very successful examples of the style. In 1951 at Chyknell, near Claverley, the celebrated international landscape architect Russell Page (d.1985) created a wonderful setting for the 19th-century house, using formal compartments framed with dark shaved yews, beech hedging and light pleached limes to frame features such as a rectangular lily pond and a rose garden (Plate 52). On the periphery more informal elements, notably a flagged courtyard and a lilac walk, were used to link the new gardens with the surrounding landscape.[16] At much the same time formal gardens were also being laid out as the setting for another old house, Longnor Hall, by its owners Colonel and Mrs. Arthur. Although, as far as is known, they were ignorant of the 17th-century Dutch garden swept away by Archdeacon Plymley in the late 18th century, the yew hedges they planted (Plate 53) picked up several of the key axes of that garden, notably the flattened raised walks. It is perhaps for that reason that they are now, in their maturity, so successful, providing a zone of regimentation and closed vistas between the house and the open parkland beyond.

Once again, the overriding emphasis of this chapter has been on the gardens and grounds of country houses. A few examples can be given, however, of smaller gardens which stand out as having been designed. One of Church Stretton's best houses is Scotsman's Field, adjoining Rectory Wood, designed in the Arts and Crafts style by Ernest Newton in 1908. Behind, the ground falls away, and here Newton laid out a series of balustraded terraces and stairs whose formal rhythm emphasised and complemented the vernacular character of the long, low, pebble-dashed house.[17] A different problem faced the architect Basil Stallybrass in 1910 when he was brought in to redesign the gardens of The Old Bell House at Ludlow, which occupied an awkward triangular plot on the banks of the River Teme. Stallybrass's solution was to create a series of levels, retaining walls, paths and steps which divided the garden into a series of compartments including a formal rose garden below the house and a Yew walk above the river.[18]

One of the most interesting results of recent work on the county's historic parks and gardens has been the discovery that the celebrated garden designer Gertrude Jekyll worked in Shropshire.[19] In 1919 she was in her mid 70s, her final book, *Colour in the Flower Garden*, having been published eleven years previously. Nevertheless, Miss Jekyll was still busy with commissions, many as memorials to men killed in the 1914-18 war. The key to her work in Shropshire lies in her notebooks, which are kept at Godalming Museum, in Surrey. Here, in envelope 25 of the archive, are Jekyll's own handwritten notes, made in July and August 1919, for a garden for Mrs. Thompson at Chesterton, near Bridgnorth (Plate 54). These give lists of plants, with the prices of each and the number required, arranged border by border. Those borders are (the letters are those given by Jekyll):

A	Border facing N. by side of tennis lawn
B	Border facing west
C	North garden: long border by building
D & E	North garden, already planted
F-M	North garden

It is not known whether the garden was ever executed, although the likelihood is that it was, or at least in part. The notebook entries concerning A-C are heavily annotated both in black ink and in red crayon, with alterations to the type and number of plants required as well as short red marks which suggest agreement with the original suggestion. Against the planting lists for beds D-M, however, there are very few annotations, although boxes were drawn around a few specific planting suggestions: four concerning marigolds, three where *Laurus tinus* had been suggested, and one to plant a Ceonothus.

All efforts to identify Mrs. Thompson have failed. She does not appear to be listed in any Directory or other printed source as a resident of Chesterton, and none of the senior members of the Shropshire branches of the Thompson family were able to suggest who she might have been. That she, rather than Mr. Thompson, commissioned the garden may indicate she was a widow, and as has been noted above, many of the gardens designed by Miss Jekyll in this period were memorials to men killed in the Great War. The difficulty in documenting Mrs. Thompson may be explained if Mrs. Bradburn, a local resident who has lived in Chesterton since the 1920s, is correct in her memory that at about this time a Mrs. Thompson took a house at Chesterton as a summer tenant. Such a tenancy would tend to leave little trace, other than in the estate records, which do not appear to have survived the sale of the estate in 1928.

The vendor of the Kingslow and Chesterton estates in 1928 was Major Richard Sidney Wilson, of a Black Country brewing family. The sale particulars provide the sole documentary clue about the location of the Jekyll garden, as only two of the three large houses in the village had a tennis lawn, such as is mentioned in her planting notes. One was Marinden House, the other Chesterton Farm. Chesterton Farm is Mrs. Bradburn's home, and it was that which she believed had been tenanted, before she came to live there, by Mrs. Thompson. At the moment, therefore, the balance of probability is that it was Chesterton Farm which was the subject of Jekyll's 1919 commission.

Chesterton Farm has two areas of gardens. The smaller lies immediately north of the house, enclosed by an angle of the house, old brick walls, and to the west by the road leading to the church. Immediately south of this, and crossed by the path to the front door, is a small lawn. Decorative single wooden gates (see below) lead from the road to the path to the front door, and from the lawn to the north garden. The main garden lies along the south side of the house and of ranges of old brick farm buildings which run east from it. Low box hedges divide the garden into compartments and edge paths. On the south side of the garden is a two-storey brick summerhouse with a pyramidal tiled roof and, on the south side, a door at first floor level approached by a short flight of stone steps. It is probably of the later 18th century.

Apart from the two noted above at Chesterton Farm several of the other gates in the village employ the same common vocabulary of diagonal slatting in their upper parts, some also having decorative wooden gate posts. The designs are very reminiscent of those produced by Sir Edwin Lutyens (d. 1944), with whom Miss Jekyll collaborated professionally from 1891 until the 1920s. There is no evidence of his involvement at Chesterton, but it remains a possibility that through Miss Jekyll gates of a Lutyenesque character were constructed for estate buildings in the hamlet.

Few garden buildings of note were built in Shropshire in the 20th century, an octagonal Classical temple at Hatton Grange, Shifnal, designed about 1960 by Clough Williams Ellis being a rare exception.[20]

On the whole it was not until the late 19th or early 20th century that most towns in Shropshire were provided with parks or recreation grounds. In the east Shropshire coalfield philanthropists gave land for such at Dawley in 1901 and at Wellington in 1910, while in the later 1920s there were several schemes, such as those undertaken at Oakengates by the Miners' Welfare Fund and at Dawley under the direction of the vicar, whereby pit mounds and other waste ground were levelled and converted by voluntary labour.[21] Private benefactors were also to the fore in other towns including Church Stretton, where the lord of the manor gave land for a park in the years before the First World War.[22]

A history of parks and gardens in the county would not be complete without mention of Percy Thrower, the first, and probably still best known television gardening expert.[23] He came to Shrewsbury in 1946 to become the borough's Parks Superintendent and to face an immediate problem in the Quarry. Here the limes in the avenues were now some 250 years old, over-mature and indeed downright dangerous; limbs and whole trees were liable to crash down in hard weather, and their number had declined from 416 in the early 19th century to 346 in the 1880s. Despite the patent decrepitude of so many of the trees there was widespread opposition in the town to the proposed mass felling, as indeed there was to Thrower's proposal to replant not with avenues but with clumps. In the end common sense prevailed; clear felling did take place, and between 1946 and 1952 the avenues were replanted, albeit with a wider, and healthier, spacing between the individual trees. Now, fifty years on, the Quarry looks much as it did in the later 18th century, and remains one of the great glories of the town.

Among professional nurserymen especial mention must be made of Henry Eckford, 'The Father of the Sweet Pea.' Born in Midlothian in 1823, Eckford worked as a gardener on various Scottish estates before moving to England in 1847. In 1874 he became head gardener to Dr. Sankey, a noted Gloucestershire plant breeder, and here first began to improve the traditional sweet pea, winning a Royal Horticultural Society First Class Certificate in 1882 for his Bronze Price variety. Soon afterwards he moved to Shropshire, to a post with more scope as assistant to Dr. Hunt at Boreatton Park, but in 1888 set up in his own right in Wem. At first he operated from a house on the corner of Noble Street and Market Street, with 10 acres of nursery ground on the Soulton Road. Later, the demand for his seeds become so considerable that he had to purchase the adjoining

*Fig. 67:
The Quarry about
1949, with felling
in progress.*

Fig. 68:
Henry Eckford (right), pictured in July 1905
in his Wem sweet pea garden with
W. Atlee Burpee, an American seedsman.

three houses in Market Street to accommodate the warehousing and packing operations. In all he probably raised upwards of two hundred varieties of sweet pea, and was awarded the Victoria Medal of Honour, the highest accolade the R.H.S. can bestow. He died in 1905.[24]

Also first offered commercially in Shropshire was the modern hybrid lupin, which was developed in Yorkshire in the 1920s by George Russell. In 1935 his stock was purchased by Jimmy Baker and moved to Baker's Nursery in Boningale, and it was from there that the flowers were first marketed.[25]

In both world wars food shortages provided an enormous fillip for gardening and especially for organized societies. Ludlow provides an excellent example.[26] Here, as everywhere else, the lessons hard learnt in 1914-18 were remembered as war loomed; a Gardens and Allotments Association

Fig. 69:
A gardening class
at Whixall Council School
about 1900.

*Fig. 70: The play equipment in Shrewsbury's Quarry in the 1950s was made
by Charles Wickstead & Co., of Kettering (Northants.), England's main manufacturer.*

was founded, the County Council was persuaded to provide more allotment ground, and lectures were given by the County Horticultural Adviser. For four years beginning in 1942 annual flower and vegetable shows were held, attracting up to four or five thousand visitors. However, just how much that interest was born of necessity was shown by the way that within just a few months of the of war's end and of the last show the Association faded out of existence. Shrewsbury saw a similar turn of events: allotments proliferated, appearing in Copthorne, Coton Mount, South Hermitage, Sundorne Road, and elsewhere. A special experimental plot was cultivated in the Quarry, a good part of which otherwise was ploughed up by the Corporation in order to grow vegetables for a British restaurant.

Many wartime gardeners would have had their first experience of gardening while at school. From the 1880s, ahead of the Technical Instruction Act of 1889 which empowered schools to provide post-school agricultural education, the county council made small attempts to provide agricultural training, and in 1885 gardens were created at a number of elementary schools. The number soon expanded as the idea of vocational training gained acceptance, and grew further during the First World War as food shortages developed.[27] Photographs survive of several such gardening classes, at Baschurch, Cardington, Newport, and Whixall,[28] showing well tended beds and well equipped boys. In the last quarter of the 20th century new trends began to emerge in the provision of public open spaces and parks. In recreation grounds there was an increased emphasis on safety: the long-established play equipment - the slides, bucking horses and jazzes - was replaced by safer, often multi-activity alternatives, and tarmac was superseded by bark or rubberized surfaces. However, may at the same time were reduced in size, and the same was true of school and company playing fields which shrank as increasing financial pressures led their controlling authorities to sell off parcels of land for development.

The creation of so-called country parks, golf courses and water recreation facilities in the same period provided no real compensation for that loss, as while recreation grounds were generally in or close to residential areas the new attractions usually lay at some distance from them. They served, moreover, very different markets, and it would not be an over simplification to observe that at the same time that recreational opportunities for the affluent and mobile sections of adult society were increasing they were diminishing for the children of less well-off families.

The most notable of the new parks created in the county in the later 20th century was undoubtedly Telford Town Park, which with a fair measure of success combined the traditional municipal playground and landscaped garden with large areas of informal country park. Laid out in the mid 1970s on 182 hectares of largely derelict land between Dawley, Stirchley and the town centre, the Town Park provided a much needed facility and focus in what for long after Telford's designation was a town centre of shops but little else. The most formal sections of the park lie at its north end where the Chelsea Garden was created with gazebo, water, summerhouse and rose gardens, based on entries made in 1977-9 by the Development Corporation to the celebrated London flower show. Nearby are the Maxell Cherry Garden, given to Telford by its first Japanese company, established there in 1983, and a garden designed for partially sighted and disabled people, with scented plants, boulders, and a bubble fountain.

One other form of designed landscape which became increasingly common in the 1980s was the golf course, and nationally it was estimated that there was a need for some 675 new courses.[29] Since the 1920s there had been instances, as at Aston Hall, near Oswestry, where golf clubs had taken over parkland and in some cases, such as Decker Hill, near Shifnal, the Hall too as a clubhouse. In the 1980s, however, the rate at which clubs were founded took off and in Shropshire new facilities opened at more than half-a-dozen locations including Allscott, Worfield and near Ellesmere. Many more were considered by speculators, as evidenced by the number of outline planning permissions sought. Although there was undoubtedly a demand from players for those new courses, more generally public opinion began to be critical of the landscapes which the design consultants created, which in the worst cases were alien, artificial and completely uninformed by the historic landscapes which they replaced. Greater sensitivity was shown towards the natural world, and in 1989 the Nature Conservancy Council (now English Nature) joined with the Royal and Ancient Golf Club to publish guidelines about how 'golf and wildlife can exist together.'[30]

Fig. 71: Sunniside, Coalbrookdale.
The Darby's house, photographed about 1860 and showing the small deer park.

Epilogue

Especially once you leave the main roads converging on the county's main towns, the Shropshire countryside retains a far more traditional character than many of England's more populous, southern and eastern counties. Thousands of acres remain parts of aristocratic estates and, as with their ancestors over many centuries, the policies of the great landowners like Lord Barnard, Lord Forester, and the Earl of Plymouth do much to mould the Shropshire countryside.[1] At the heart of most of those estates is still a country house, although not always occupied by the owner if indeed, in at least one case, at all. From the later 19th century, and with hindsight since the onset of the great agricultural depression in the 1870s, the expectation, even social necessity for the aristocratic landowner to maintain a great house and a lifestyle based on it to match has tended to decline alongside the income from his estate. As owners became further burdened with death duties and by the cost of labour, houses tended to become an oppressive encumbrance, unsaleable other than for their materials, and prey for the demolition contractors; in 1955, during the worst decade for loses, it has been estimated that in England as a whole one country house was being demolished every two and a half days.[2] In Shropshire, Oteley, Shavington, and Sundorne, to name but three, were felled at about that time, while what was left of Tong Castle was blown up. Among the houses that survived the trend has been for them to be separated from their land, and to become the homes of families whose main income derives from something other than farming or agricultural rents.

But whatever the fate of a house, in most cases its historic park generally still makes a considerable beneficial contribution to the local landscape, whether or not it retains a formal identity. Lodges, park boundary walls and fences, and perimeter tree belts add variety and interest to roadside scenery, while specimen trees, even when now isolated in farmland, often make significant contributions to the countryside. That tends to be especially so where, as in much of north Shropshire, the landscape is relatively flat, and the fields large and straight edged. Here the height and profile of mature trees provide variety and intimacy as well as a haven for wildlife in what can otherwise be very open, even bleak and featureless, landscapes.

At the moment the amount of legal protection which historic landscapes enjoy against destruction or damage, whether by new roads, housing, industry or leisure facilities, is generally very limited indeed. The nature and degree of any protection offered is also unpredictable, reflecting the hotch-potch way in which planning law has evolved. Individual buildings and archaeological monuments remain far easier, legally, to safeguard than more extensive historic landscapes, a framework for whose protection still seems a long way off. Within some parks or gardens one or more structures, which can range from a summerhouse to balustrading or even ornaments, may be designated as Listed Buildings, which cannot therefore be altered, developed or demolished without the consent of the Secretary of State. On the other hand repair or conservation work on them may be eligible for grant aid, and in recent years English Heritage has made substantial contributions on that basis towards the repair of the Bird House and Rotunda at Badger Dingle and the summerhouse at Blodwell Hall. Parks and gardens, or more usually parts thereof, may also contain archaeological sites Scheduled as Ancient Monuments: a prehistoric farm or Roman villa invisible to the naked eye, or perhaps the 'humps and bumps' of a settlement and its fields removed when the park was created. Very few gardens are Scheduled in their own right. Others still may lie within Conservation Areas of special architectural or historic interest, where planning consent is required for works which would otherwise be regarded as permitted development. Tree Preservation Orders are obviously also relevant and can give protection to avenues, clumps, shelter belts or specimen trees.

Under the National Heritage Act of 1983 formal recognition at least was given to the specific importance of historic parks and gardens with the instruction to English Heritage to compile a Register of those of 'special historic interest.' For Shropshire the original Register, compiled in 1986, contained 27 sites; several have been added since then, and as more is discovered about individual sites that number will probably creep upwards, although not dramatically. As with Listed Buildings they are graded I, II* or II to denote their relative importance. Registration (unlike the Listing of historic buildings or the Scheduling of ancient monuments) offers no legal protection to parks and gardens but does make them 'material considerations' in any planning decision. This means that planners must weigh up the historic significance of any Registered landscape touched on by a planning application and may, on that basis, recommend its refusal or amendment.

Ultimately, however, all conservation is dependent upon public support, and none of the above measures offers protection against the actions of the criminally wilfull or the genuinely ignorant. Public support is also needed where more active, dynamic, conservation is required. Many landscapes are now over mature, and have seen little if any maintenance or phased renewal over many decades, or even perhaps since an initial planting in the 18th or 19th centuries. Lakes become clogged, paths disappear, and buildings collapse. Left unmanaged woodland tends to become overgrown, especially with self-sown species such as ash and sycamore, and will begin to creep outwards from its intended margins with discrete blocks tending to coalesce obscuring the unity of the park. But however much required to arrest such a decline the 'judicious use of the axe', to use Repton's phrase, always tends to attract opposition. Again, a better understanding of the issues involved and of the nature of the historic landscape, as well as the fact that felling will be followed by effective management and perhaps even replanting, would go some way to qualifying what is often an emotive rather than a rational reaction. With parks and gardens, which can be subtle and fragile landscapes, that support will only be forthcoming if there is a better and fuller appreciation of the range and diversity of the resource, and of the contribution they make to the countryside in general and especially to the setting of some of its finest historic buildings.

Notes and References

Abbreviations

English Heritage, *Register* - English Heritage, *Register of Parks and Gardens of Special Historic Interest in England: Shropshire* (1986 and amendments)

N.C.C. -   Nature Conservancy Council

N.L.W. -   National Library of Wales, Aberystwyth

N.M.R -   National Monuments Record, Swindon

N.R.A. -   National Register of Archives

P.R.O. -   Public Record Office, London

S.M.R. -   Shropshire Sites & Monuments Record, Environment Department, Shropshire County Council

S.R.R.C. -   Shropshire Records and Research Centre, Shrewsbury

Stamper, *Survey* - P.A. Stamper, *A Survey of Historic Parks and Gardens in Shropshire* (Shropshire Archaeology Unit Report 41,1993)

Stamper, *Compendium* - P.A. Stamper, *Historic Parks and Gardens in Shropshire. A Compendium of Site Reports...1994-6* (Shropshire Archaeology Service Report 55, 1996)

V.C.H. - Victoria County History

Introduction

1. *Victorian Gardens* (1986)
2. *Georgian Gardens: The Reign of Nature* (1983)
3. Stamper, *Survey*
4. Stamper, *Compendium*

Chapter 1: Medieval and Renaissance

1. F. Barlow (ed.), *The Life of King Edward the Confessor* (1962), 40. See also *ibid. 52.* For a discussion see Barlow's *Edward the Confessor* (1978), 131
2. T. Rowley, *The Landscape of the Welsh Marches* (1986), 149
3. *V.C.H. Shrops.* 4 (1989), 42
4. For para. *ibid.* 43
5. *Ibid.* 1 (1908), 493
6. *Ibid.*
7. Ibid. 2 (1973), 67 (corr. *ibid.* 3 (1979), 398) 84
8. *Ibid.* 1, 489
9. *Ibid.* 11 (1985), 42

10. Toulmin Smith (ed.), *The Itinerary of John Leland... 1535-1543*, 4 (1909), 2
11. O. Rackham, *The History of the Countryside* (1986), 39
12. *V.C.H. Shrops.* 4, 43
13. *Cal. Inq. Misc. 1392-9*, pp. 112 et seq.
14. R.R. Davies, *Lordship and Society in the Marches of Wales 1282-1400* (1978) 119-20
15. S.M.R., SA 570
16. *Cal. Pat.* 1313-17, 250
17. *Ibid.* 1330-4, 134
18. *Ibid.* 1292-1301, 383
19. *Ibid.* 1334-8, 448
20. *V.C.H. Shrops.* 1, 495
21. S.M.R, SA 3507
22. S.R.R.C. 837/50-1
23. B. Ross, 'The Accounts of the Talbot Household at Blakemere...1394-1425' (Canberra Univ. M.A. thesis, 1970), 88 (copy in S.R.R.C.)
24. M. Watson and C. Musson, *Shropshire from the Air* (1993), 68
25. Vernacular Architecture 24 (1993), 57; *V.C.H. Shrops.* 10 (forthcoming)
26. For useful synopsis G. and S. Jellicoe *et al*, *Oxford Companion to Gardens* (1986), 438-41
27. S.R.R.C. 330/12
28. Watson and Musson, *op.cit.* 69; survey and interpretation by Paul Everson, Royal Commission on Historic Monuments (England)
29. TS. supplied by Jeffrey West
30. C. Platt, *The Great Rebuildings of Tudor and Stuart England* (1994), 52-60
31. Report in Stamper, *Compendium*
32. For Eyton see S.R.R.C. 6001/226, ff. 50-65
33. *V.C.H. Shrops.* 8 (1968), 39
34. S.R.R.C. 322/1/1; W.R. Wilson-North, 'Formal Garden Earthworks at Moreton Corbet Castle', pp. 225-8 in *Brit. Archaeol. Rep.* 209 (1989)
35. *Trans. Shrops. Arch. Soc.* 4 ser. 4(1914), 311
36. W. Cathrall, *The History of Oswestry* (1855), 264-5; S. Leighton, *Shropshire Houses Past and Present* (1901), 25
37. Discussed below
38. *V.C.H. Shrops.* 11, pl. 50
39. *Country Life*, 23 July 1898, 82
40. See R. Strong, *The Renaissance Garden in England* (1979), 215-19
41. *V.C.H. Shrops.* 11, 216 and pl.
42. English Heritage, *Register*, G62
43. Letter, 27 Aug. 1783, Phillip Williams, gardener, to Mr Plimley of Longnor, in N.L.W., Pitchford Hall (uncat.) colln. Ref. owed to Mr James Lawson.
44. Inf. from James Lawson; *Trans. Shrops. Arch. Soc.* 4 ser.7 1918-1918, 188

45. *Salopian Shreds and Patches* 1 (1874), 9
46. Report in Stamper, *Compendium*
47. C. Sinker et al, *Ecological Flora of the Shropshire Region* (1985), 12; B. Henry, *British Botanical and Horticultural Literature before 1800* (1975) i, 193-8; *Garden Hist.* 9 (1981), 99-109. Rea was well known at Hanmer: *ibid.* 16 (1988), 3-4
48. For this para. Henry, *op.cit.* 193-9
49. *Country Life*, 23 June 1977, p. 1736
50. S.R.R.C. scrapbook C04/4106, p. 24
51. An amusing description of a visit to Boscobel in 1792 is provided in D. Souden (ed.) *Byng's Tours* (1991), 202-3
52. P.R.O., C2/Jas. 1/T3/14 (ref. owed to Dr Peter Edwards)
53. S.R.R.C. 972, bdle. 233, item 1
54. *V.C.H. Shrops.* 8, 81
55. P.R.O., C104/22, pt. 2 deed (ref. owed to Dr D.C. Cox)
56. Below, next chapter
57. *Trans. Shrops. Arch. Soc.* 9 (1886), 203
58. Lambeth Palace Libr., MSS. 700, f.115; 702, f.37; 707, f.64; 708, f.227
59. J. Peake, *Ellesmere, Shropshire* (1889), 39
60. E. Hopkins, 'The Bridgewater Estates in Shropshire in the First Half of the 17th Century' (M.A. thesis in S.R.R.C.), 56-7
61. T. Rowley, *The Shropshire Landscape* (1972), 122
62. Preliminary report by P.A. Stamper, copy in S.M.R. (SA 7753)
63. Leighton, *op.cit.* 3
64. Report by P.A. Stamper, copy in S.M.R. (SA 7669)
65. *Trans. Shrops. Arch. Soc.* 65 (1987), 70-4
66. P.R.O. STAC 2/24/234 (ref. owed to Dr Peter Edwards)
67. *Country Life*, 16 Aug. 1946, 303-5
68. *V.C.H. Shrops.* 10
69. Stamper, *Compendium*; *Garden Hist.* 12 (1984), 86
70. M. Faraday, *Ludlow* (1991), 178
71. For transcript of second edition see *Trans. Shrops. Arch. Soc.* 2 ser. 4 (1892), 241-63
72. Inf. From Mr James Lawson. See also B. Champion, *Everyday Life in Tudor Shrewsbury* (1994), 37-8, 79
73. John Gardiner, d.1628, probably his son, was commemmorated in St. Mary's church with a brass which called him (John) 'Horti Cultor' : *Trans. Shrops. Arch. Soc.* 2 ser. 4 (1892), 241-63
74. See Henry, *op.cit.* 68-9

Chapter 2: The Age of Formality:
1660-1750

1. For the paintings (current whereabouts unknown) H.A. Tipping, *English Homes* IV (i), *1649-1714* (1929), 151-4. Mid 19th-century copies by F. Stackhouse Acton held at the Dower House, Longnor, 1994.
2. For what follows Stamper, *Survey*, 327. Mr James Lawson is thanked for the original ref. there cited.
3. At the Hall 1995
4. D. Jacques and A. Jan van der Horst, *The Gardens of William and Mary* (1988), 99
5. Report in Stamper, *Compendium*
6. *Ibid.*
7. Staffs. R.O. D1287/3/4. Thea Randall is thanked for supplying details.
8. M. Watson and C. Musson, *Shropshire from the Air* (1993), pl. 7
9. T. Williamson, *Polite Landscapes* (1995), 26
10. S.R.R.C. 3424
11. S.R.R.C. DP 587
12. Inf. From Annie Bannerman, Shropshire Conservation Development Trust
13. H.E. Forrest, *Some Shropshire Houses* (1924), 65
14. Report in Stamper, *Compendium*
15. *Ibid.*
16. Below
17. I. Edwards, *Davies Brothers Gatesmiths* (1977), 52-5, 83, 86. The other Shrops. example of their work is the gates at Oswestry church, of 1738: ibid. 48
18. English Heritage, *Register*, G52
19. *V.C.H. Salop.* 11 (1985), 216 and pl. 48; S.R.R.C. 1224/1/2
20. Report in Stamper, *Compendium*
21. *Ibid.*
22. *Ibid.*
23. Below
24. S. Garbet, *The History of Wem* (1818), 251
25. For background to what follows see *Trans. Shrops. Arch. Soc.* 56 (1957-60), 34-48
26. *Hawkstone: Rescue of a Masterpiece* [1987]
27. S.R.R.C. 112/1/2710
28. *Ibid.* /2709
29. *Ibid.* /2715
30. *Ibid.* /2717-18
31. *Ibid.* /2502, 2513
32. *Ibid.* /2747
33. *Trans. Shrops. Arch. Soc.* 56 (1957-60), 47
34. S.R.R.C. 1121/1/2502
35. *Trans. Shrops. Arch. Soc.* 56 (1957-60), 47

36. For the date see *The Gardener's Chronicle* 11 Dec. 1880, p.748, where a recent 120+ year tree-ring count was reported.
37. *Country Life*, 130 (1961), 502-3, 558
38. F. Leach, *The County Seats of Shropshire* (1891), 216
39. *Country Life*, 141 (1967), 1449-50
40. Report in Stamper, *Compendium*
41. C. Morris (ed.), *The Journeys of Celia Fiennes* (1949), 226
42. Inf. From Mr James Lawson citing *A Complete System of Geography* (1747) which was based on 'all that is useful in the 4th and last edition of The Complete Geography of Hermon Moll'.
43. *Shropshire Notes and Queries* 5 (1896), 109 (ref. owed to Mr Bill Champion)
44. Photos in S.R.R.C. Mr A.M. Carr is thanked for pointing these out.
45. R. Morriss and K. Hoverd, *The Buildings of Shrewsbury* (1993), 93
46. *Trans. Shrops. Arch. Soc.* 4 (1881), 111-12, citing Pennant, *Tours in Wales* (1810), i, 20
47. Draft paper on Quarry by P.A. Stamper
48. See watercolour of Quarry (above, pl. 20) in S.R.R.C. showing it without avenues but with two couples of 'the quality' walking along the river's edge.
49. *Trans. Shrops. Arch. Soc.* 9 (1886), 203
50. I. Watkin, *Oswestry* (1920), 76-8
51. Morris, *op.cit.* 226
52. Staffs. R.O. D1287/3/4. Thea. Randall is thanked for this ref.
53. Above
55. *Shrews. Chron.* 8 Apr. 1775, p.5 col. 3; 17 May 1777, p.2 col.4 (refs. owed to Mr W.E. Jenks)
56. S.R.R.C. 552/temp. box 179/3
57. Heref. and Worc. R.O. (Heref.), Heref. Dioc. Rec., inv. of Ric. Benthall 1720
58. S.R.R.C. 1224, box 164, list of garden goods
59. *Trans. Shrops. Arch.* Soc. 2 ser. 7 (1895), 113
60. S.R.R.C., Watton's Cuttings vol. 6, 336
61. J. Harvey, *Early Nurserymen* (1974), 69
62. C. Burne, Salop. Folk Lore (1883), 101
63. S.R.R.C. 112/2780
64. N. Stockton, *Castle Bromwich Hall Gardens* (1988), 19;112/2780 22. Wright was among the subscribers to Miller's *Gardener's Dictionary* published in 1731: inf. from Mr James Lawson
65. Staffs. R.O. D1287/3/6B
66. For refs. *see* Stamper, *Compendium*
67. Harvey, *op.cit.* 95

68. S.R.R.C. 'Parks and Gardens' research file, corresp. 1971
69. Inf. from Mr Bill Champion
70. Copy of inventory kindly supplied by Dr B.S. Trinder
71. P. Stamper, *'The Farmer Feeds Us All'* (1989), 52
72. *Trans. Shrops. Arch. Soc.* 9 (1886), 205

Chapter 3: A Taste for Views and Wind:
1750-1820

1. For Morville see Stamper, *Survey*
2. M. Batey and D. Lambert, *The English Garden Tour* (1990), 181-5
3. Harris, 'A Lifetime of Service' (TS., 1981) (copy in S.R.R.C)
4. English Heritage, *Register*, G49
5. *V.C.H. Shrops.* 10 (forthcoming)
6. Stamper, *Survey*, 291
7. Report in Stamper, *Compendium*
8. S.R.R.C. 3182/1, f.2
9. I am grateful to James Lawson for discussing Sundorne with me.
10. F. and K. Wood (eds.), *A Lancashire Gentleman* (1992), 64-5
11. A. Morton, *The Trees of Shropshire* (1986), 75
12. Report in Stamper, *Compendium*
13. M. Symes, *A Glossary of Garden History* (1993), 33
14. *A Description of Hawkstone* (1832), 11; *ibid.* (1850), 18
15. Listing descr.; photo in S.R.R.C.
16. *Hawkstone, A Short History and Guide* (1993)
17. *Hawkstone: Rescue of a Masterpiece* [1987], 3.5
18. J. Higgs, *The Land* (1964), caption to pl. 111
19. Cited by T. Williamson in *Polite Landscapes* (1995), 81
20. Report in Stamper, *Compendium*
21. D. Souden (ed.) *Byng's Tours* (1991), 201-2
22. D. Stroud, *Capability Brown* (1975), 172, 235
23. Report in Stamper, *Compendium*
24. S.R.R.C. 731, box 225, divorce papers
25. Williamson, *op.cit.* 83
26. Report in Stamper, *Compendium*
27. S.R.R.C. 552/9/207/2-3; 552/9/295/12 ; P.R.O., C109/71-8, boxes 74-5
28. Report in Stamper, *Compendium*
29. S.R.R.C. 4068/6; *V.C.H. Shrops.* 8 (1968), 42; inf. from Mr W.E. Jenks
30. G. Jackson-Stops, *An English Arcadia* (1992), 104-6
31. P.R.O., MP AA 2
32. Plan in private hands: inf. from Mr Julian Gibbs
33. S.R.R.C. 3127
34. G. and S. Jellicoe *et al*, *Oxford Companion to Gardens* (1986), 161
35. Inf. from Mr James Lawson
36. S.R.R.C. 6000/13192

37. *Ibid./*19530
38. *Ibid./*13192
39. C. Gotch, 'A Shropshire Vogue: Notes ... Relating to Roberty Mylne' (TS., copy in S.R.R.C.). For Halston see also report in Stamper, *Compendium*
40. *V.C.H. Shrops.* 10
41. Jellicoe, *op.cit.* 15
42. N.R.A., Report on Pitchford MSS., item 205
43. Below, next chapter
44. English Heritage, *Register*, G50
45. Reports on Walcot and Hardwick in Stamper, *Compendium*
46. English Heritage, *Register*, GD 2262
47. H. Colvin, *Biographical Dictionary of British Architects* (1995), 293 and corresp. in hands of V.C.H. Shrops.
48. N.R.A., Report on Pitchford MSS. items 108, 169
49. S.R.R.C. 552/8/121
50. Jellicoe, *op.cit.* 333
51. The National Trust, *Attingham Park* (1987), 37
52. Biog. details from Jellicoe, *op.cit.* 467
53. G. Carter et al, *Humphry Repton Landscape Gardener 1752-1818* (1982), 161; S. Daniels and C. Walker (eds.), *The Picturesque Landscape* (1994), 80-7
54. Carter, *op.cit.*
55. *Trans. Shrops. Arch. Soc.* 65 (1987), 64-9
56. The National Trust, *op. cit.* 39
57. *Architectural Review* (Aug. 1976), 96-100. For the lodges hereabouts see T. Mowl and B. Earnshaw, *Trumpet at a Distant Gate* (1985), 87, 161-2
58. The National Trust, *op. cit.* 23
59. H. Colvin, *Biographical Dictionary of British Architects 1600-1840* (1978), 682
60. Report in Stamper, *Compendium*
61. B. Botfield, *Stemmata Botvilliana* (1858), ccxxxi
62. Vol. 2
63. Report in Stamper, *Compendium*
64. S.R.R.C. 4133/2
65. *Trans. Shrops. Arch. Soc.* 65 (1987), 70-4
66. Report in Stamper, *Compendium*
67. *Ibid.*
68. *V.C.H. Shrops.* 10
69. Thus dated in Mowl and Earnshaw, *op.cit.* 47-8
70. Report in Stamper, *Compendium*
71. C.B. Andrews, *The Torrington Diaries* (1936) iii, 232-3
72. S.R.R.C. 4068/6
73. Andrews, *op.cit.* 241
74. Inf. from Mr James Lawson
75. Daniels and Walker, *op.cit.* 22
76. Report in Stamper, *Compendium*
77. *Life in the English Country House* (1978), 256
78. *Montgomeryshire Coll.* 34 (1907), 47;

79. report in Stamper, *Compendium*
79. *A Description of Hawkstone* (1832), 6
80. Report in Stamper, *Compendium*
81. S.R.R.C. 800/bdle. 142/1
82. S.M.R., SA 04285
83. S.M.R., SA 01002
84. Girouard, *English Country House*, 262
85. For a brief summary of the bathhouse see A.E. Brown (ed.), *Garden Archaeology* (1991), 132
86. S.R.R.C. 398/1
87. Andrews, *op.cit.* iii, 232-3
88. S.R.R.C. 398/1
89. S.R.R.C. 552, box 103, acct. of payments by John Rolls... to March 1790; *ibid.*, to Lady Day 1791
90. S.R.R.C. 515/2, pp. 263-79
91. Deduction based on archit. evidence
92. Report in Stamper, *Compendium*; S.R.R.C. 552/9, design for hothouse
93. Report in Stamper, *Compendium*
94. S.R.R.C. SC/1/51
95. Reports in Stamper, *Compendium*
96. S.R.R.C. 6000/13667
97. K. Pritchard, 'To maintain an independent English country gentleman: the role and relationships of Thomas Barnfield, steward of the Apley Park Estate' (M.A. dissertation University of Keele, 1994), 31-2
98. S.R.R.C. 5492/1-2
99. K. Thomas, *Man and the Natural World* (1983), 211
100. S.R.R.C. 3315/Ti/3, p.4 at end
101. *Ibid.*
102. *Ibid.*, p.6 at end
103. *Staffordshire Studies* 6 (1994), 34, citing Staffs. R.O., Aqualate Colln. 45/6
104. *Shrews. Chron.* 11 Nov. 1829, p.[2]
105. Para. on Quarry based on draft paper by P.A. Stamper
106. S.R.R.C., Cooper & Co. (Broseley) cat., p.186
107. D. Lloyd, *Ludlow Castle* [c. 1990], 10
108. G. Lipscomb, *Journey into South Wales... in ...1799* (1802)
109. As shown on an engraved view
110. Andrews, *op.cit.* iii, 242
111. A. Raistrick, *Dynasty of Ironfounders* (1953), 221-2
112. *V.C.H. Shrops.* 11 (1985), 36. For various descrs. See B. Trinder, 'The Most Extraordinary District in the World' (1988), s.v. Rotunda
113. Ironbridge Gorge Museum Libr. photo 1984.6496
114. S.R.R.C. 1987/64/6, pp.8-9, 14, 51, 65, 70
115. Trinder, *op.cit.* 6

Chapter 4: A Return to Formality: 1820-80

1. For what follows see report in Stamper, *Compendium*
2. M. Batey and D. Lambert, *The English Garden Tour* (1990), 276-8; B. Elliott, *Victorian Gardens* (1986), 79-80
3. G. and S. Jellicoe et al, *Oxford Companion to Gardens* (1986), 211
4. A convenient source for the following para. is B. Henry, *British Botanical and Horticultural Literature before 1800* (1975), ii, 159-62, 476-8. See also *V.C.H. Shrops.* 10 (forthcoming, Acton Scott).
5. S.R.R.C. 2906/1
6. For his sub. etc. see S.R.R.C. 2563/50, June 1812
7. S. Pieberga, 'William Salwey Gilpin (1762-1843). A review of his work as a landscape gardener' (Univ. York, Inst. Advanced Archit. Studies D. Phil., 1995), ii, 320; S.R.R.C. 731, box 256, corresp., 29 Aug. [1832], Gilpin to [Sir Rowland Hill]. Dr. Pieberga is thanked for inf. on Gilpin.
8. Elliott, *op.cit.* 33, 36, 50, 61-2, 118; M. Hadfield et al, *British Gardeners: A Biographical Dictionary* (1980), 134
9. Pieberga, *op.cit.* ii, 320, citing Keele Univ. Libr., Sneyd Coll. SC19/180, corresp. Gilpin to Ralph Sneyd 1 Sept. 1832
10. *Ibid.* SC13/127 and 13/132. In 1898 it was said the gardens were laid out 'about 1839': *Country Life*, 23 July 1898, 80
11. Pieberga, *op.cit.* citing W.S. Gilpin, *Practical Hints Upon Landscape Gardening* (1835 edn.), 46 [and nb. not in 1832 edn.]
12. Report in Stamper, *Compendium*
13. Gilpin, *op.cit.* 46
14. Report in Stamper, *Compendium*
15. 7 June 1890, p. 709. See also *Eddowses's Shrewsbury Jnl.* 28 Apr. 1886, p.5
16. Report in Stamper, *Compendium*
17. Plans at Willey Hall 1994
18. Report in Stamper, *Compendium*
19. *Ibid.*
20. *Ibid.*
21. H.M. Auden, *Notes on Condover* (1932), 25
22. Photo in S.R.R.C. 5735
23. Elliott, *op.cit.* 130-2
24. *Country Life*, 23 July 1898, 80
25. Stamper, *Compendium*
26. Burford report in Stamper, *Compendium*
27. *V.C.H. Shrops.* 11 (1985), 140; F. Leach, *The County Seats of Shrops.* (1891), 275
28. *Trans. Shrops. Arch. Soc.* 4 (1881), 315. I am grateful to D. Lloyd for drawing my attention to this.

29. Hawkstone, of course, had earlier had a menagerie, and in 1852 Hill had sought to acquire wild turkeys and other fowl from the U.S.A.: *Hawkstone: A Short History and Guide* (1993), 26; S.R.R.C. 731/11

30. C. Lever, *They Dined on Eland* (1992); section on eland in S.R.R.C. 731/11

31. Following based principally on Listing descrs.

32. *V.C.H. Shrops.* 10

33. Report in Stamper, *Compendium*

34. Listing descr.

35. For Ludstone, Stokesay and Ruckley *see* Stamper, *Compendium*

36. *V.C.H. Shrops.* 11, 257: S. Bagshaw, *Directory of Shropshire* (1851), 437

37. S.R.R.C., Chitty file 764/1-10; SC/1/21; Watton's Cuttings vol. 2, p.498

38. See A. Desmond and J. Moore, *Darwin* (1991), 10-13; J. Brown, *Charles Darwin* (1995), 15. I am grateful to Mrs. Susan Campbell for bringing the garden book (in private hands) to my attention.

39. Jellicoe, *op.cit.* 123

40. Inf. from A.M. Carr, who is thanked, based on poll bk. 1826 and burgess election recs. For Watton *V.C.H. Shrops.* 3 (1979), 263, 312-13

41. S.R.R.C., Watton's Cuttings vol. 1, p. 315 (ref. owed to Mrs D. Haxton)

42. H.E. Forrest, *The Old Houses of Shrewsbury* (1911), 36

43. Report in Stamper, *Compendium*

44. B. Trinder, *The Darbys of Coalbrookdale* (1978), 66

45. S.R.R.C. 5735, photo *c.* 1870; *V.C.H. Shrops.* 11, 40

46. S.R.R.C. 1987/64/6, p. 37

47. He died in 1862 'from the effects of falling through a gap in the floor at the opening of the International Exhibition' in London: *D.N.B.*

48. Viator, *Guide to the View from Brimstree Hill* (1885); J. Randall, *Shifnal and its Surroundings* [1879], 52

49. F. Brighton, *The Story of Great Ness* (priv. print. 1933), 9; inf. from Mr Nigel Jones, S.C.C.

50. S.R.R.C. neg. B232

51. S.R.R.C., Watton's Cuttings vol. 12, cutting for Aug. 1854

52. J.W. Nankivell, *Chapters from the History of Ellesmere* (1983), 44-5; S.R.R.C. 2013/162-3

53. B. Trinder, 'The Most Extraordinary District in the World' (1988), 122; J. Randall, *Tourist's Guide to Wenlock* (1875), advertisement

54. H. Conway, *People's Parks* (1991)

55. *V.C.H. Shrops.* 11, 212

56. S.R.R.C. 4001/Admin/8, box 65

57. Inf. from John Powell, Ironbridge Gorge Museum Trust librarian

58. Copy in Ironbridge Gorge Museum Trust Library

59. Conway, *op.cit.* Appendix One; 8 & 9 Vic. c. 118, ss. 15, 30

60. *V.C.H. Shrops.* 4 (1989), 176-7

61. *Eddowes's Jnl.* 27 Sept. 1848, p.[4]

62. *Ibid.* 31 May 1848, p.[2]

63. N. Rowley, 'The Baschurch File' (TS., priv. print, 1994; copy in S.R.R.C.), 14

64. S.R.R.C. 780/Pa/5-10

65. I. Watkin, *Oswestry* (1920), 292-3

66. *Trans. Shrops. Arch. Soc.* 2 ser. 11 (1899), 153

67. Photos in Much Wenlock Museum

68. Bagshaw, *op.cit.* 675; *V.C.H. Shrops.* 3 (1979), 160

69. Present by early 1890s. Inf. from David Lambert

70. *National Trust Studies 1980* (1979), 10-20

71. S.R.R.C., Watton's Cuttings vol. 1, p.104

72. Desmond and Moore, *op.cit.* 61

73. *Salopian Phoenix,* 23 July 1842, 5 (copy in S.R.R.C.)

Chapter 5: Milner, Jekyll and Page: 1880 Onwards

1. Sotheby's, *Stokesay Court Sale Cat. 28 Sept.-1 Oct. 1994,* into. See also report in Stamper, *Compendium*

2. At Stokesay Court 1995

3. Report in Stamper, *Compendium*

4. M. Girouard, *Life in the English Country House* (1978), 315-16

5. Report in Stamper, *Compendium*

6. *Ibid.*

7. *Shropshire* (1958), 331

8. B. Elliott, *Victorian Gardens* (1986), 172, 196

9. Report in Stamper, *Compendium*

10. Stamper, *Survey,* 463. There are docs. relating to garden in S.R.R.C. 4763/2

11. *Country Life,* 16 Aug. 1946, 304-5; English Heritage, *Register,* G44

12. W.H. Godfrey, *Gardens in the Making* [1914], fig. 61; S. Leighton, *Shropshire Houses Past and Present* (1901), 39

13. Stamper, *Survey,* 199

14. *The Gardener's Magazine,* 7 June 1913, 413-13

15. At Attingham Hall

16. B. and A. Palmer, *Some Shropshire Gardens* (1990), 17-18; Stamper, *Compendium*

17. *V.C.H. Shrops.* 10

18. C. Brooks, *Some Histories of Ludlow's Secret Gardens* [1995] (copy in S.R.R.C.)

19. Report in Stamper, *Compendium*

20. Listing descr.

21. *V.C.H. Shrops.* 11 (1985), 112, 212, 290

22. *V.C.H. Shrops.* 10 (forthcoming)

23. Para. based on draft paper on Quarry by P.A. Stamper

24. B. Jones, 'Henry Eckford' (TS.; copy in S.R.R.C. class BE 39vf) and inf. correcting acct. from Mr. Good

25. *Shrews. Chron.* 5 Jan. 1951, p.4; *The Field,* July 1987, pp. 62-3

26. F. G. Reeves, *Ludlow in Wartime* (1981), 22-4

27. *V.C.H. Shrops.* 4 (1989), 265; R. Hill and P. Stamper, *The Working Countryside* (1991), p. 128

28. Photos in S.R.R.C. and author's collection

29. Quoted in Shropshire County Council Strategic Sports Review 1990-2000 (1990)

30. N.C.C., *On Course Conservation. Managing Golf's Natural Heritage*

Epilogue

1. For the great estates' fortunes in 20th cent. see *V.C.H. Shrops.* 4, 250-6

2. J. Harris, *The Artist and the Country House* (1996), 23

List of Figures

Black and white plates, unless otherwise attributed, are by the author

List of Plates

Unless otherwise attributed all plates are by the author. A list of standard abbreviations precedes the footnotes and references on page 115.

Index of Persons and Places

Places in Shropshire are followed by a four-figure grid reference;
places outside are located by their historic County.

More books on Shropshire's history and gardens published by Shropshire Books

Everyday Life in Medieval Shrewsbury £7.95
Dorothy Cromarty

Everyday Life in Tudor Shrewsbury £7.95
Bill Champion

The Farmer Feeds Us All £4.95
Paul Stamper

Monastic Shropshire £2.50
George Baugh and David Cox

Shropshire From The Air £13.99
Michael Watson and Chris Musson

Some Shropshire Gardens £3.99
Barbara and Alan Palmer

For a complete list of Shropshire Books titles please write to:

**Shropshire Books,
Column House,
7 London Road,
Shrewsbury,
Shropshire SY2 6NW.**